EXECUTIVE
MOTHERHOOD

ASHLEY QUINTO POWELL

To all the breadwinning, butt-kicking powerhouse women out there, especially my mother.

Contents

Introduction   vii

Yes, Richard. Women can have it all.   1
You don't have to Get Stuff Done   15
You Don't Have Imposter Syndrome   35
Why is it so hard to pay women?   47
In Pursuit of the Trophy for Mom of   67
the Year
Working Moms Do it Better   81
Change starts with you, Friend.   95
The Fix   103

Acknowledgments   117
Before You Go   119

Introduction

Several years ago I came across a photo of a pool float that looked exactly like a gigantic menstrual pad. If you were *trying* to make a pool float that looked like a feminine hygiene product, it wouldn't be this true to life. And the joke, of course, is that if there had been a woman—a *single* woman—at the table, this could have been avoided.

Sally Ride got sent into space for six days with 100 tampons. The Apple Health Kit came out and didn't have a period tracker. Across the board, medical testing is done on men. Women are seen as too complicated or something, and eh, if this medication works on men, it will probably work the same way on women. No problem.

This is funny, but it gets dark quickly.

In tech, there's a serious shortage of women in the boardrooms, in the design rooms, and on the development teams. Artificial intelligence systems are notorious for adopting the biases of the people who create them, and this is nowhere more true than in the case of gender biases. For example, facial recognition programs often misidentify women or assume someone with a Dr. prefix is a man. More alarmingly, we're seeing many, many instances where Internet of Things devices are being used as tools for stalkers and abusive domestic partners.

One reporter asked 11 family tracking apps if they could be used to track a partner without their knowing —and eight said "Yes." The author of that article surmised that those app developers might have seen that as a *positive* feature, not a bug. In fact, that might have been the point of the app in the first place.

Women need to be in the room.

And that includes women who are also moms. I'm a Mom of two and I've always been the sole, primary, or majority breadwinner.

I believe that women should get to choose whether to work or stay home. Personally, I want you to stay in the workforce for the sake of all women, but if you've made or are making the decision to stay home, I get it—100%.

I'm also a big believer in a household where one parent works and one stays home. If you're afforded that incredible privilege, you should not feel bad about taking it. Women of color have traditionally been completely excluded from the privilege of staying at home, and I'd like to see that change, in particular.

I just want there to be an equal number of stay-at-home moms and stay-at-home dads.

Let me back up. If you and I were having this conversation on March 1st of 2020, I would tell you that this is *the* time to be a working mother. We're seeing awesome systemic change and things are looking nothing but up.

The discussions that we were and are having around diversity, equity, and inclusion are good for everyone in the workforce, and the market was slowly shifting. We started seeing women at the top of more organizations, and the men at the top were slowly, very slowly, starting to reclaim some of their home lives—publicly. We saw Alexis Ohanian, the co-founder of Reddit, and Mark Zuckerberg, and Chance the Rapper all take very public paternity leaves.

When men do that, they create space for parental leave to be something that's not just for women, and to leave behind the so-called "mommy tax"—the loss of income over the life of a mother's career and her diminished likelihood of advancement.

I've spent most of my career in tech, and that's a fascinating place to be. There's a very serious shortage of diverse voices at tech companies. And to address that, tech companies are having to overcome their biases and be very creative about the benefits they offer, so we're seeing things like unlimited vacation time and paid volunteer time. There's even a Chicago company that administers IVF reimbursement as a benefit.

My own career and homelife have been a study in throwing aside assumptions and being creative. For starters, let me say that I have a VERY handsome husband—and that he was a stay-at-home dad for five years, and for part of that time, I commuted to Chicago from my home in Madison, WI. That's not unusual—not in my industry.

What was unusual is that I am a mom of young kids.

Occasionally, I got negative feedback. One business acquaintance told me he wouldn't consider himself a good parent if he didn't see his kids every day. His goal was to be home for dinner every night, like clockwork.

This man also wore fancy vests everywhere, so we don't need to take him too seriously.

But more often than not, I would meet another woman who'd instantly understand the appeal. She could tell that I was able to work and be productive and get lots accomplished, and then come home for glorious and fun-filled three-day weekends. And those women would always look a little wistful and say, "That sounds amazing."

And it was.

I am not one of those mothers who secretly wants to be a stay-at-home mom. I knew that before COVID.

And I know that in my bones, post-COVID.

For years now, I've been very loud about my role as a working mother. Since 2015, I've given talks and workshops on salary negotiation for women, which is important. But it's especially important to me since I've been the sole or primary breadwinner for most of the years I've had kids, and the idea that my family isn't making as much money simply because I'm a woman is ludicrous.

At the end of 2019, I gave a TEDx talk on what I've termed "Executive Motherhood," which is the intersection between the upward trajectory of a woman's career and the moment when she has her first baby—and who she becomes as she continues her upward climb.

Our childbearing years come exactly as we're really making traction in our careers. We hit our stride. We start to climb up a corporate ladder, we're finally making money in ways that feel substantial, we are starting to grow into positions of power. And all of a sudden, we have to make a full and complete stop.

Instantly, our bosses think we're less dedicated. We have to plan ahead for someone to do our job in the meantime which, while completely necessary, lets us know just how quickly we can be replaced. At best, whatever upward trajectory we were on becomes a year-long plateau. It's awful to watch the hard work you've put into your career go temporarily up in flames. And it's not much better at home.

When I took my first maternity leave, I was having a record year at a job I adored. I couldn't wait to have long, boozy lunches with friends. We would coo at my adorable baby, asleep in a pram. It seemed like an exciting vacation.

The reality was a bit different than I had imagined. I had no one to have lunch with; everyone I knew was at work.

Truthfully, I was bored to tears. My son was adorable and delightful—and mostly asleep. Breastfeeding made me feel like a gigantic udder. My brain was atrophying. I had gone from a dynamic, vital woman to a giant bored boob.

When my son was about four months old and I had just gone back to work, I was expecting to pick up exactly where I left off. I felt like I was supposed to be in a groove, but I wasn't. My husband and I were fighting. We had yet to acknowledge the postpartum elephant in the room. I was still a giant boob. And I thought to myself, *I do not know why people do this.*

And the thing is, I didn't mean work. I meant I didn't understand why people *have kids.* That time was so devoid of joy for me, it was so hard and so lonely. I wasn't feeling the fulfillment that so many parents feel, and I honestly just didn't get what was supposed to be so great about parenthood.

Well, lots of mothers go through a difficult time at this stage. In addition to all the pressure to perform like you always have at work, there are also the needling little voices in our heads—and sometimes very real voices, in real life—that say, "Well, it *would* be better for your family if you stayed home." And husbands say, "Well, honey, I make pretty good money and I'll be up for a promotion soon, why don't you stay home?"

And that can be really tempting. If you don't have serious drive, and really serious support, you're not going to make the decision to stay at work. What initially feels like a giant sigh of relief ultimately becomes the exchange of your career for your husband's. With a wife at home taking care of everything *but* work, he'll have the opportunity to concentrate on nothing else. Now, if *that* guy doesn't have upper management written all over him, I don't know who does.

There's a strong business case for making sure companies look like the communities they serve—and that includes parents. So it's too bad when companies and individual managers assume that parents are less dedicated or less qualified. In fact, parents are statistically more productive workers.

Who is the *most* productive, you might ask?

Moms of two children. Take that, singletons.

Corporations need to start paying more attention to the baby-shaped part of their leaky executive pipelines. Mid-career, emerging leaders are often the same folks who feel stable enough in their careers to put down roots and start families.

More than that, moms *want* to be here. There is a strong bias in corporate America that suggests mothers are less dedicated and less ambitious, but mothers are, in actuality, more likely to have upper-management ambitions.

In 2020, we lost over two million women in the workforce because female-held jobs were more likely to be furloughed, and the demands of working and caregiving became ten times more challenging. But whether a woman leaves the workforce because of the added challenges of a national pandemic, or she leaves at a normal time for the completely normal reason that she wants to have children, she'll see the negative effects of taking time off for years to come.

We tend to focus on the immediate loss of income when a woman takes maternity leave, but there are consequences for her contributions to Social Security and her 401k that will reverberate for decades.

Carolyn Leonard, a Chicago legend in the financial space, has estimated that a three-year break from the workforce results in half a million dollars in lost income over a woman's lifetime.

Here's another really alarming statistic: In 2019, only 2.7% of venture capital funding went to women. We're not in the room when the decisions to fund are being made so we're not getting the funding. That definitely means that opportunities for change or improvement are being lost because the people who could make it happen just don't understand.

A great example of this is an entrepreneur friend of mine in Michigan. She came up with the idea for a women-only co-working space with drop-in childcare years ago. She's in Grand Rapids. Not Chicago, or New York, or LA. In a big city, you can get very niche and still capture a sizeable population.

But in Grand Rapids, they didn't get it. They told her there wouldn't be enough women who found value in a co-working space like this. And she asked for funding over and over and over again... And when she finally put together enough money to open a location, she was booked up immediately.

Now this will come as absolutely no surprise to a mom. She was able to open up a second location right away, and is serving a need in her community that desperately needed to be filled—but that all the men with venture capital couldn't even see.

We need to be in the room.

Over the past decade, I've been an advocate for women, especially moms.

Once they have kids, there's a gentle push for career-driven women to step back, slow down, or leave the workforce altogether. I felt it personally—and I pushed back.

I had my first child as my career was really taking off. That was no accident. I finally felt stable in my position as a senior leader at a large consulting firm. My income could support a family. My life was humming along beautifully, and I wanted to have children with the lumberjack hunk I married.

Until I had kids, I didn't even feel like a real adult. I was just masquerading as a fully-grown human, genuinely surprised that I was pulling it off well enough to qualify for a mortgage.

Children were a symptom of success, and I had no intention of slowing down.

So I was surprised when my colleagues and bosses started treating me—and my ambitions—differently.

When I looked around for other high-level moms, there weren't shining examples of how to balance or thrive. Frankly, there weren't even a lot of examples of graceful surviving.

So I started pulling all the ambitious mothers together for a conversation that, at this point, has lasted years. *How do I juggle all this? How do I advance my career? How do I call on my partner to do more? How do other people get any sleep?*

I've learned many lessons the hard way. I fought for my ambition to take up space in my life, to push ahead, and to stay front-and-center.

I've learned many lessons the funny way—and I hope you'll laugh along with me in these pages.

Women need to be in the room. We need to be at the table.

We need to be *at the top.*

So now let's talk about how we get there and stay there —and how companies can protect the investments they've made in their workforce.

Yes, Richard. Women can have it all.

Whoever fed us the line that we can "have it all" was up to something.

Years ago, I was binge-watching that show with the Duggar family (who have approximately 47 children but no television), and I got twitchy-angry at a scene where their oldest was talking to his new wife about her getting a job outside the home.

To paraphrase, he told her, "Yes, absolutely, go ahead, but make sure that you also do everything you already do around the house and don't expect me to help around the house or do anything differently." So you can see why I was twitchy-angry. That's about the *least* supportive thing he could possibly have said.

Poor girl.

But isn't that basically what all women have been told? Perhaps not explicitly, but statistics don't lie: Pre-pandemic, women shouldered the majority of household chores and were more likely to stay home. Of course, during the pandemic, it was largely women who stepped back from work and stepped up to childcare—and if we didn't quit, we did both.

Sister, if you did both, someone owes you a bajillion dollars, because that was tough.

When the pandemic hit, I was headed to Washington, D.C. to have dinner with Hillary Clinton... at a gala with roughly 1,500 other people.

For the previous two years, I split time between Madison and Chicago. First, I went there because I landed my "Big Dream Job" and my husband didn't want to move. And then, when I started consulting, so many of my professional contacts and clients were in Chicago that I just kept at it. I loved having a whole city to work in and a whole city to play in.

My husband had been a stay-at-home-dad and was keeping everyone happy and healthy on the home front, and in Chicago, I shared a fabulous apartment with my oldest friend in the heart of Boystown. It was perfect.

And then *everything* changed.

My husband, wanting better health insurance and reliable income, got a job at the post office. He loved it, but it's an incredibly demanding job, and at that time, there were labor shortages and an avalanche of Amazon deliveries as everyone else sheltered in place.

There are a few ways to say my husband is a postal carrier.

He's a mail escort.

My children look a lot like the postman.

But I digress. He was working six days a week and long hours each day. My kids were doing remote 4k and 1st grade. And I was trying to keep my consulting business afloat.

Almost immediately, I went from being a successful, high-performing working woman with everything humming, to an overwhelmed work-at-home-mom with everything falling apart.

I won't dwell on how awful that was. You were there, too, likely with your own horror story of pressure and overwhelm.

A year before, my buddy, Mo Cheeks, hitched a ride with me to Chicago. Mo and I have known each other for years because we both work in sales for tech companies, but most people know Mo because, for a long time, he was on Madison's City Council. Mo made a run for mayor and although it wasn't successful, he's still in my phone as 'Mayor Mo Cheeks.'

When Mo started his mayoral campaign, his wife had just had their second baby. When his campaign ended, he was abruptly without a job and home with his wife and kids… all the time. When he expected to pick up exactly where their dynamic had left off, his wife sat him down and had a frank discussion. They needed to learn to be a family of four, she said, because she'd spent the past year feeling like a single mom of two. She was happy to support him, of course, but the three of them were in a groove that he wasn't a part of. Their family needed to do some work to get into a new dynamic that had space for all of them.

I had this story in my mind for most of the early pandemic. Because the same thing was happening to me.

Our lives were upside down. Dad, who had been home, was now at work almost all the time. Mom, who had only been there for weekend fun times, was now the teacher, caregiver, and disciplinarian. And instead of running my business with time to think and network and plan, I was stuck in a basement office with diminished capacity and no idea which way was up.

Because of this conversation with Mo, I knew to be patient with my family. I knew when to ask for their patience. I knew I couldn't walk in assuming I was CEO of the house when I'd only been a frequent visitor before.

And I was keenly aware that my relationship with my kids was getting turned on its head. As a four-day commuter, I had been interacting with my kids like a really fun divorced dad. Since our time was limited, it was always packed with excitement. We would regularly go to restaurants where everyone else was celebrating a birthday—because the kinds of restaurants we went to regularly were reserved for special occasions in other families.

To move forward, you've got to let go.

This was not the first time my family had gone through a major transition and I have seen this lesson play out every time.

When my kids were babies and my husband and I were both working, my mother moved in to help with childcare. The first thing she did was rearrange my kitchen. It's hard not to know where anything is in your own house, but if I wanted my mother's help, I needed to let go of my control of the kitchen.

If you don't think you'll be able to give up control, let me introduce you to my orange living room.

When I started spending four days a week in Chicago, my husband was left with the tremendous responsibility of caring for our home, kids, and dog—alone. I knew I was going to have to be ok with things not being done exactly the way I would have done them —which was fine when we were just talking about which way the toilet paper should roll, but very different when it comes to home decor.

When I started commuting to Chicago, my husband painted our living room *orange*.

And, yes, it's the orange you're hoping it's not. You wouldn't call it Blaze Orange, but you might call it Bright Pumpkin or Sunset Traffic Cone.

Is it awful? No. It's a compromise.

You don't have time to do everything. As much of a powerhouse superhero as you are, you need to delegate little stuff so you can focus on the stuff that matters.

It's hard to give up control over something you think you can do better, or more efficiently, or the right way, but you don't actually have time for that nonsense. Delegate what you can and go about your business making the world a better place. Or making gobs of money. Or building an empire.

I promise that's a much better use of your energy.

My kitchen got rearranged again when I hired a nanny. I make peace with not ever being able to find the damn cheese grater because I want to achieve goals that have nothing to do with my kitchen.

We need to get out of the mindset that we have to do it all.

In my work as a consultant, I help people drive growth and revenue for their businesses. I know exactly how to make someone successful, but they have to do the work. Time and time again, I see otherwise successful, capable people bogged down with minutiae that need to be done but don't drive revenue.

When my business was just a baby business, I hired a virtual assistant, and it was the single best decision I made that year. I didn't have much money, so I told her to keep it under $300 a month. I needed help staying on top of my email, scheduling meetings, and making my business look more professional. Between Chicago and Madison, my schedule was a nightmare and emails had always been the bane of my existence. She helped me stay on top of that so I could do business development and client work—the things that really made me money. And with whatever hours were left over, my VA slowly plodded through making my proposals look amazing, my website redesign, and a branded slide deck for presentations.

I believe there are two universal pieces of advice that apply, no matter the circumstance:

1. You need a breath mint.
2. You need a virtual assistant.

A breath mint is always a good bet. And a virtual assistant is always more helpful than you think they're going to be.

I started a VA agency earlier this year to solve all the problems I'd helped clients work through as they hired their own VAs. It's hard to give up control, and it's hard to accept that there are other ways to do things that aren't the way you'd do them. But if you insist on handling all the little stuff, you're going to live your life scrambling to get the little stuff done and never get to the big, audacious goals you've set for yourself.

As part of my research for the VA agency, I interviewed lots of incredibly high-performing people, and asked how they think about delegation. One of those interviews was with Amiel Harper, a lawyer by trade and a visionary by nature. The amount of things he accomplishes in a day is incredible—he is literally changing the world around him.

He told me that you think of your business as a baby. It's hard to have someone else hold your baby—but you have to. At some point, you need a nap and a shower. You don't throw someone your baby and run away. You build trust, get to know them, and slowly get comfortable enough to walk away, confident that your baby is safe and well cared-for. The same is true for team members. It's important to communicate, build trust, and get confident upfront.

Your work is important, Amiel said. And it deserves to be in the world. Ask yourself, "Is this CEO work?" If it's not, find someone else to do it.

We should all be the CEO of our own work. It's tempting to wear all the hats but you only have one head.

At home, women often get trapped in project management land. We tend to carry the brunt of the mental load of the household, and as much as our partners are helpful, they're rarely carrying their fair share.

I'll bet good money that you know most of these things about your house:

- How much toilet paper you have.
- How long until you need to buy more dog food.
- Which groceries your family needs every week.
- When the bathrooms were last cleaned.
- What you'll eat for dinner tomorrow.
- What your social plans are for the next three weeks.
- The names of three babysitters you can call on Saturday.

There is an enormous mental toll to knowing and managing all the moving parts that make a family run smoothly.

At work, we know that project management is its own role. It's someone's whole job and it's a tough one, at that. So why, then, do we take on project management at home as if it's a part of who we are?

Early in our marriage, my husband and I used to get into the same fight over and over again. I would say, "I need help!" and he would respond, "I'm happy to help. You just need to tell me what to do!"

It's not ok to live with someone who can't take it upon themselves to start the laundry when socks are low or pick up the living room before company arrives. You need someone who also understands what needs to be done and does their fair share.

It's not help we need. It's a partner who can pull their own weight.

If you've ever gotten stuck in the cycle of counting everything that you are doing and comparing it against everything your partner is doing, you know it's a losing battle. You end up bitter and resentful and no matter what either of you does, it's never good enough.

My husband Sean and I got out of that cycle by looking at everything like a game we had to win *together*. We're a team and we win or lose together.

I'm grateful to have such a wonderful and supportive partner. I'm grateful for what he does and the effort he puts in. But I don't thank him for his "help" anymore—it's not the "help" I'm grateful for. I'm grateful he's such a good partner. So that's exactly what I tell him.

Thank you for being a good partner. And for being so incredibly good-looking. And dat butt.

I talk publicly about being a working mother quite a lot, and semi-frequently, a woman will tell me all about their own stint as an executive working mother a decade or two ago.

One woman told me that ahead of a week-long business trip, she hustled to make and freeze all the meals her family would eat while she was gone, get schedules together so her husband would know which kid had to go where, and wash and fold all the laundry so no one would run out. It was everything she would have done in the whole week packed into a couple of days. When she got on the plane, she told me, she passed out cold and woke up in her destination city having no recollection of the flight.

That, she believed, was the only way her family would survive the week without her.

It sounds awful.

I'm confident her husband would have stepped up, but he didn't even have a chance. What does it say about a man who can't be trusted to step in and handle the care of his own family for a single week?

That's going to be a hard pass from me, boss.

In stark contrast, I spoke to a woman who served as a circuit court judge while her three kids were growing up. Her husband had an equally demanding job. They hired a nanny to be there when the kids got home from school and to make and serve dinner. This woman was half-apologetic about it. Not everyone can afford a luxury like that and she was conscious that it seemed incredibly indulgent. But her time with her kids was at a premium and with this arrangement, she was able to be present and enjoy the time they had together.

Friend, the world needs you to do Big Things. Hard Things. Incredible Things. We're not served by the belief that our families can't function without us. Our partners deserve the chance to be our teammates. And our kids deserve to see a great partnership in action.

Bottomline: Do the CEO work. Delegate everything else.

Join the conversation.

How are you delegating so you can be amazing today? What could you do if you had five extra hours in a day?

Post your response on Linkedin, tag me (Ashley Quinto Powell), and use the hashtag #executivemotherhood.

You don't have to Get Stuff Done

American women are tough—especially midwestern women. We pride ourselves on being able to run companies, raise babies, and organize the church potluck without breaking a sweat. Time and again, we're hard at work being the one who gets more done than the rest of the team combined. How many times have you heard a woman leave a job and have to be replaced by two (or more) people? We're proud of our ingenuity and our ability to accomplish 10x more than the next person.

Finally, how many times have you heard a woman talk about how she's the one you call when you want to Get Stuff Done?

Picture, if you will, my friends Richard and Betty. They do the same job at similar companies and everything should be equal. But, of course, we know it's not.

Betty arrives early in the morning after having wrangled the two-kids-to-school circus. She works her tail off, often without a break. She eats lunch at her desk while she coordinates dental appointments, and leaves 10 minutes early to relieve the nanny and wrangle the family-dinner-and-bedtime-routine circus. It's a grind, but Betty's confident that her hard work is recognized. She's got a great husband at home who's plenty helpful and her children are the light of her life. She's efficient and delivers great work.

Richard arrives at work at 9am still sweating a bit from his morning run. He spends some time chatting before easing into work. He eats lunch with coworkers and chats up boss-types over mid-afternoon coffee. He stays late to finish the work he started and returns home to dinner with his beautiful wife and kids. He makes a point of always being home for dinner and kissing his kids goodnight. It's the life he always dreamed of and he knows he's on track for a great career.

When Betty thinks about it, she knows she's performing at a higher level than Richard. You know what? Let's call him Dick. He's spending time on frivolous social stuff she doesn't have time for. She's getting more done in less time and even if they're delivering the same quality of work, she does it faster. Only a woman could wrangle the kid/home circus and still be an all-star at work the way she is. Only a woman could be more efficient, have more going on personally, and be harder working than Dick, and still be thought of as performing at the same level.

You know where this is going. Dick is in line for a major promotion; likely to make double the salary; and even more likely, Betty will be there to congratulate him when it happens, along with everything else she does.

Betty's going to spend a lot of time congratulating *herself* on the sheer volume of tasks she's able to accomplish in a day. The classic Peggy Lee song comes to mind.

> I can wash out 44 pairs of socks and have 'em
>   hangin' out on the line
> I can starch and iron two dozen shirts 'fore you
>   can count from one to nine
> I can scoop up a great big dipper full of lard from
>   the drippins can
> Throw it in the skillet, go out and do my
>   shopping, be back before it melts in the pan

'Cause I'm a woman! W-O-M-A-N, I'll say it
again

But we're missing the point.

When we organize our personal brand around being the woman who gets stuff done, we *believe* we're saying that we're the one you bring in when you need the cavalry. When you're up against impossible deadlines and unreachable expectations, when you need an outright miracle, you call me.

That's not what our boss hears. Our boss, unaware that the expectations of the job are unreachable and the deadlines are impossible, simply understands that we're doing our job. Not above and beyond. Not orchestrating miracles. Not building Rome in a day.

We're basically saying, "Congratulations to me—I meet your minimum expectations!"

...Huzzah, I guess?

No one bothered to tell the higher-ups that they've asked for something unreasonable. That might have been you, but you were too busy being silently superhuman.

We believe we add so much value by being the one who gets it done because we see our colleagues doing frivolous things we wouldn't dream of doing. They're spending time chatting it up at the water cooler. They're going for drinks after work. They're kicking off early on Friday to go play golf.

We wouldn't dream of doing any of that nonsense because that's not how you Get Stuff Done and anyway, we're late to pick up the kids as it is.

But all that social nonsense isn't frivolous—it's networking. It's building and maintaining a community for the times when you need to land your next job, find clients, or call in a brilliant and trusted advisor.

Our amazing work ethic is killing us.

We're stuck in the trap of being a heads-down lone wolf who does (unrecognized) great work but lacks the community that might lift us up and help us along the way—either by making the current journey easier or by opening doors to the next one.

You need *to* network because you need *the network*.

Instead of being superhuman, putting your head down, and pulling off the impossible, tell them it's impossible and build a network.

Inevitably, there are items on your to-do list that aren't your job. I'm talking about all those extra tasks that no one else does but that don't move you or your career forward. Planning the office holiday party? Being your own admin? Mindless, repetitive tasks? Drop it, delegate it, automate it.

Open up your time for big, strategic thinking and building a network that can help you get where you're supposed to go.

Your network is going to help you land your next role. Your network is going to help you piece together a brilliant strategy. Your network will provide you with collaborators for a big project. They're the folks who will talk about you when you're not in the room and recommend you when they need a ringer.

Create an army of champions.

The energy that you put into building a network will pay off tenfold and it's infinitely less exhausting than doing the work of three people.

Me? I have wonderful and robust networks... but it wasn't always this way.

When my then-boyfriend (now husband) and I moved to a new city together, we spent a whopping seven years without making friends outside of work. To be fair, Sean and I were both in demanding jobs and in the honeymoon phase of our relationship; we were busy paying dues in our careers and falling in love.

Once I got pregnant, however, I didn't fit in well at work. There were very few women in the office and even fewer moms. I had tried so hard to be considered "one of the boys," but no one wants to go for after-work beers with a woman who's visibly pregnant. You never know when she's going to mention her nipples.

I needed a community in a different way than I had before. I needed women who could validate my experience, who could offer advice, and who wouldn't have a coronary if someone mentioned her mammary glands.

I started meeting people in moms' groups and at networking events and ventured into many rooms where I didn't know a soul. To this day, the best and most basic networking technique I often use is to remember that everyone was a dork in high school.

Everyone, at least once, has been there: You're standing in a cafeteria, alone and unpopular, holding your lunch tray like a schmuck, hoping desperately that someone will have mercy, lock eyes with you, and wave you over to their table. It's a universal experience and if you're lucky, it only happened once before you vowed that as God is your witness, you'd never be unpopular again.

If you look carefully, you can see people reliving that exact experience like a trauma flashback at the edge of every networking event. She's clutching a glass of warm Chianti and trying to look busy on her phone. He's checking his watch and calculating the earliest moment he can leave and still get credit for attending. Those are your people. If you don't know anyone in the room, find those two poor saps, lock eyes, and invite them to sit at your proverbial table.

> A really great network is made up of people who are excited to help one another get where they're going.

Keep an eye out for the following people:

The Mentor: She's been there and she's done that, but she's not jaded. She gives you solid advice and challenges you to be the best person you can be. She's going to call you out on not thinking big enough, so buckle up. You might not have a formal mentor-mentee relationship with her, but she's going to change your life.

Several years ago, I was having lunch with my friend Jennifer, and I was telling her about this amazing company I was interviewing with. They were in Chicago, two and a half hours away from my home in Madison. But my husband was desperately dropping hints that he didn't want to move to Chicago. He hates Chicago. He grew up an hour and a half outside of the city in a vacation town that gets bombarded by wealthy Chicagoans from Memorial Day to Labor Day. As they head to their summer homes, his hometown goes from quaint and quiet to completely overrun. I'd have gotten a better reception if I'd suggested we move to a war zone.

Jennifer asked me, "Why don't you commute? Get an apartment in Chicago and work there four days a week, and come back on the weekends." It's actually very common in the tech industry. Consultants do it all the time. But it hadn't even occurred to me because traveling for work was not something *moms* do. That advice changed my career and I commuted, happily, for two years, stopping only for a global pandemic.

The Connector: I love the connector. She knows everybody, and she wants you to know them, too. If you're new to networking, she'll spin you up a dozen connections. All you have to do is ask. Real estate agents and financial advisors often make the best connectors because it's a brilliant sales strategy. When she makes connections, she gets to stay top-of-mind and sets the precedent that you refer people back and forth, so make sure you return the favor.

One of the best connectors I know is a woman named Alida. Her client list reads like a who's who of Chicago innovators and tech companies, and for good reason.

She does great work as a culture consultant, but she also makes referrals as easily and as frequently as most people breathe. It's incredible. She once got a thank-you note from a friend detailing how Alida had helped her land a C-Suite position with a company she loved, and it was Alida's introduction that got her in all the right doors—but Alida didn't even remember making the introduction. It's truly a part of who she is.

The Power Partner: Someone who's in the same industry with the same clients, but doesn't compete directly. The concept of Power Partners is the brainchild of Meghann Conter and her networking group, The Dames.

As Meghann says, no one wants to be stabbed with a business card at a networking event, but you *can* build alliances with people who are already talking to the people you want to talk to. It's a recipe for all the warm introductions you can handle and you'll never have to make a cold call. It's a great strategy because you can build your network based on trust, you can share knowledge, and you can refer business to one another when it makes sense.

The Other Moms: When moms make time to network, they have to be strategic with their time, so they don't tolerate a lot of fluff. To that end, networking with other moms is efficient and fruitful, and when you need it, it's your best place for support.

My friend Sara put together a group called "Mothers Mothering One Another" because everyone needs a big hug once in a while, and no one will understand what you're going through like someone who's in the same boat. It's brilliant. There's so much comfort in being able to let your guard down. Professionally, we spend so much time pretending there's no dumpster fire in the background. We arrive at work looking calm and ready to get down to business, hiding the three hours it took to feed, clothe, and deliver everyone else to where they need to be. Your childless coworkers will never really have the right amount of appreciation for what it takes to get a four-year-old into pants. Unless, of course, they have experience putting a sweater on a rabid squirrel.

The Relentless Champion: Who do you turn to when you've had a big success? When you've done the impossible, closed the largest deal in human history, climbed Mount Kilimanjaro, or negotiated a big, fat, juicy salary increase? Who can you tell *without diminishing the accomplishment for the sake of their ego?*

We've been trained from a very early age to share credit, not to boast, and not to be full of ourselves. Well, sister, the people who said that were threatened by your greatness.

We bond when we commiserate, but that bond gets threatened when we're really crushing it.

I have the single best champion in my best friend, Lorelei. She is incredible in her own right, but her encouragement is a force to be reckoned with. It has become so motivating to me that I get measurably depressed if I go more than seven days without speaking to her.

Personally, I have an affinity for dynamic, spirited, opinionated women. Were you ever made to feel you were "too much"? You're my people. Have you ever been told to "tone it down"? You're my people. Been told you're loud? Bossy? I can spot you from a mile away and we'll know in the first five minutes that we'll be friends for life.

It's all about the mindset

A good network is, of course, filled with your people— but the hallmark of a *great* network is the mindset. Seek out people who believe a rising tide raises all boats. You want people who support you—even the ones that are traditionally your competition. There's no room for fake friendships in a great network. We need the ride-

or-die, call-me-anytime people who we know are rooting for us.

To build that network, you're going to have to ask for help when you need it.

Remember Betty and her commitment to Get Stuff Done? She's tough. She's resilient. She doesn't need help. She's got this.

Except sometimes she doesn't. We've all been there, and we don't always admit it.

I sat across from one of my favorite people for coffee the other day as she told me that she'd left her day job to concentrate on her photography business. I knew that already because I saw it on social media and was more than a little miffed that she hadn't told me herself. She's a brilliant photographer, and her help with my branding is a huge part of my own success. Her goal is to work full time for herself, and in the meantime, she said, she's doing delivery-gig work.

The thing that sits between her and her dream is getting more clients.

I was horrified. Why didn't she call me? I specialize in helping people get more clients. It's *literally* what I do. And for her, I would have been happy to book another photography session and introduce her to every woman I know in need of a spectacular headshot.

But mostly, I felt betrayed because I thought we were *friends.*

Like most of us, she's fiercely independent. She knows what she's doing. She didn't want to appear weak. She didn't want to bother anyone.

But here's the thing: Our friendships grow when we can ask for and accept help from our friends.

Shallow friendships exist where there's no rough water.

If both our lives are perfect and nothing challenging ever happens, we can meet for high tea and pat ourselves on the back for how well we're doing. We'll never grow personally, and we'll never grow in the depth of our friendship.

Imagine, on the other hand, that you're in the thick of a tough time and a friend gets *in the muck* with you. This isn't getting together for cocktails and commiserating over a bad situation, this is help that *changes* the bad situation.

Years ago, the cape came off of my supermom outfit and I needed serious backup.

I was shuttling my two young kids to school with my beloved and ironically-named Sweet Molly the Boston Terrier. Sweet Molly was anything but. She was the kind of dog that would strain on the leash, snarling at passersby. She bullied our neighbor's service dog. She jumped on children. I loved her fiercely, but looking back, I have no idea why.

While I bustled the children into school, Molly, alone in the running car, went all rabid beast on the minivan next to us, barking and jumping against the window in the way only small dogs who think they're enormous can. In the jumping and snarling, she hit the door buttons, locking up the car—with my purse, my phone, and the only set of keys to our other car inside. I called my husband from my watch and he called a neighbor who, at the drop of a hat, left work, picked up my husband and a spare set of keys, and dropped them both off, saving the day.

On the ride home, as I was expressing how truly grateful I was, I started brainstorming ways to say "Thank you." Invite him to dinner? Bake him a cake? Organize a parade? Buy him a car?

"No," my husband said, "just let him help us. That can be the end of it."

It's true. We consider this man a friend and a great neighbor. He was there when we needed him and we've been there when he needed us. That's what friendship is *supposed* to be.

Somehow, we get into such an independent, pull-yourself-up-by-your-bootstraps mindset that we miss out on opportunities to have a real relationship with people. If our friends never see us at our worst, when we're freaking out because we're not sure we'll make payroll this week, when mascara is running down our face because our marriage is in crisis, when we're exhausted and tapped out and wondering how we're going to do it another day, how will they know us at all?

You can't be friends with stock photos, so don't pretend to be one.

But wait, aren't women unsupportive of one another? Aren't women catty and competitive? Don't we stab each other in the back? Don't we pretend to be sincere and then gossip at the first chance we get?

No. It's a myth that women are unsupportive of other women.

But it comes from an honest place. We've been made to believe there's only one seat at the table and we have to compete over it. And for a long time, this was absolutely true. There was one token pink chair at the table. There was room for one woman, and if that was going to be you, you had to be sure you were the last lady standing. It's no wonder some women see one another as a threat.

We happen to be at a place of privilege today, where that is (mostly) untrue. We're standing on the shoulders of women who blazed a trail before us. But if some women are still in the habit of being defensive and competitive, it's as a result of history, not an inherent character flaw.

I don't love catty people. I believe there's enough business to go around. As I stated earlier, I believe rising tides raise all boats. But I don't blame folks who aren't there yet. We spent a long time having to compete over one pink chair, and it's a tough habit to break.

The last female boss I had was an incredibly successful VP of a big corporation, and an absolute nightmare. She practically scorched the ground she walked on. My team inherited her when two divisions combined—and she came with a reputation. Once, the story goes, she was in the middle of giving a performance review when she went into labor. She winced slightly, clutched her belly, and insisted they finish the meeting like there wasn't a child trying to escape her abdomen. She was mean, and she was ruthless. I went to one of our quarterly meetings after the best quarter my team had ever had. I left the quarterly meeting wondering if I'd have a job the next day. It was brutal. She told me how seriously she took our company's non-compete clause. Her brother had violated it, and as a result, they hadn't spoken in years.

She was tougher and less sympathetic than any of the men. She had to be. To get where she wanted to go, she had to *prove* that she wasn't weak. In male-dominated fields, there's an assumption that women can't cut it. The boys' club is the boys' club because it's messy and smelly and tough—and no place for women.

When you want to prove you deserve to be in the club, you embrace the mess and the smell and you meet tough with tougher.

Today, we feel betrayed when other women behave like this. Doesn't she know we're all supposed to support one another? Doesn't she know we lift as we rise? Wasn't she at the meeting where we all agreed to mentor and sponsor one another? But I contend we have to look, with sympathy, at women who paved the way and did what it took to claim their seat at the table.

In the future, when the world has made the changes we're pushing for now, our daughters' generation can look back at us and be fully horrified that we were paid less or that we couldn't figure out how to break all the glass ceilings. They'll know they're standing on our shoulders.

Join the conversation.

Who have been your best supporters and advocates? What would your life look like if you had champions everywhere?

Post your response on Linkedin, tag me (Ashley Quinto Powell), and use the hashtag #executivemotherhood.

You Don't Have Imposter Syndrome

My least favorite side-effect of success is when we have arrived at our dream job—the job we've strategized, agonized, and worked our tails off to land—but we feel like we don't deserve to be there.

It's a real thing, for sure. As you're interviewing, you're happy just to be considered. You're flattered that you're called back. You tell everyone it's a long shot but such an honor to even be in the running. You let yourself daydream about what your name would look like with that BIG title on a business card.

And then you get the job. Like magic, you've climbed up onto the pedestal that you've put your heroes and your mentors on. You imagine the great perks and the way people will react when they realize what a powerhouse, BIG deal you are.

You're surprised—but you're only surprised because you know your own history in its entirety. You know the whole story arc. Everyone else sees you as you are today, or maybe through the lens of how you've grown over the last couple of years, without knowing your whole history. It makes sense to the world at large that you hit your big milestone because they see the trajectory and they've shifted their image of you from kind-of-a-powerhouse to total-powerhouse and from pretty-big-deal to very-big-deal. It's not a leap.

My father likes to say that a career should be a series of lateral moves. What this means is that if you start with an entry-level position at your first company and then get promoted all the way to manager, you'd move to your second company as a manager and work your way up to Director and then VP. Then you'd move companies to a VP position at your third company and work your way up to CEO. In other words, you'd make a lateral move every time you started to feel like your career had stalled.

By his reasoning, your career stalls when people can't see your potential. When you're working your way up to manager at your first company, your bosses are patting themselves on the back for helping you advance so quickly. But they will also always see you as just the "entry-level worker." However, if you enter a second company as a manager, people can see your farther-reaching potential. They champion you all the way to VP but no further. But if you enter as a VP, it's clear you're headed to the C-Suite in a way that isn't obvious to anyone who still sees you as a plucky kid. That's why it's so rare for a janitor to work their way up to president of the company. (And why the companies that *did* promote someone from janitor to CEO will never let anyone forget it.)

But you have known yourself since you were not a big deal. You're more than aware of what a serious miracle it is to be where you are today. You remember your very first job when you couldn't get anything right. You remember all those times you were mortified to learn you'd made a huge blunder, messed up a project, insulted a coworker inadvertently, drank too much at the company holiday party. Sometimes these memories show up just to be a confidence killer. They'll appear, out of nowhere, at 4am, as you're preparing for an important meeting, just to make you cringe.

In the early part of my career, I had a job that started at 7am. On my first day of work, I showed up at 6:45 like any sensible *go-getter*. There weren't any cars in the parking lot, which was a little odd, *but who knows?*

Maybe there was a back parking lot? I thought I'd try the door and if it was locked, I'd wait in my car. I pulled it, it opened, and I walked right in.

And set off the alarm.

The door lock was on an automatic timer but the alarm was on, and whoever arrived first would turn it off. I walked in that day with all the confidence of an upwardly mobile whippersnapper to an empty office and the steady beep of the alarm. The alarm went from a steady beep to a full-on blare, and the police arrived at 6:59, along with all 80 of my new coworkers and a boss who was wondering what kind of idiot he had hired. "Didn't someone tell you to come at 8 o'clock on your first day?"

But back to you. You know your whole history, especially the not-so-flattering parts. And, let's face it, we're not trained to dwell on the parts that make us look *good.* Nope, we lay awake remembering what it's like to make an ass of ourselves in front of strangers.

It makes sense that we're surprised when we're promoted to our dream job because we're keenly aware that we're also the ones who couldn't get it together to arrive on the first day at the right time without creating a gigantic spectacle.

We know we're awkward teenagers disguised as professional humans and *that* can make us feel like imposters.

There's a statistic that women only apply for a job if they fit 100% of the criteria, while men apply if they meet 60%. And there are umpteen books and articles that will tell you that you just need the confidence to go after the job you want. See? It's that easy!

Poppycock. That statistic actually comes from a Hewlett Packard internal report made famous in Sheryl Sandberg's book, *Lean In*. Ms. Sandberg goes on to talk about a mindset shift women need to make to go after jobs we think we can do by learning on the job. She recommends that we not be so concerned about being ready for the "Big Job," and that if you want that "Big Job" you can learn as you go.

This suggestion seems fair enough, but it's still not the complete picture.

More often than not, we don't get the jobs we're applying for.

The *Harvard Business Review* published a study that found that if there's one woman in a candidate pool, she has statistically no chance of being hired. None. With two women in the consideration set, her chances rise more than 79%.

Let's look at this using the example of our plucky friend, Betty. Betty has a career trajectory that's clearly pointed way up and the next step is a director-level position. She's confident in her abilities, excited about the future, and ready for the added responsibility. So she starts applying all over the city. She'll be applying for jobs she meets all the qualifications for, but if she's the only woman in the candidate pool, she's not getting hired. Especially because the higher the position, the less likely there is to be another woman in the consideration set. But, of course, she doesn't see that. From her vantage point, she's qualified and ready and excited and confident... and still not getting the job.

At best, she'll go on lots and lots of interviews. My bet is that recruiters will throw her in the mix to make sure there's a woman in the candidate pool. If she can hang on and keep interviewing and keep her confidence up, at some point she'll be lucky to land the director-level job of her dreams.

Poor Betty! She won't enter that position with the confidence she had at the beginning of her search. She'll feel lucky to have made it in the door.

And if that was her experience getting a director-level position, what are the chances she'll take a chance on a VP position she *doesn't* meet all the criteria for?

Statistically, we are more likely to be fired, less likely to be hired, and less likely to be promoted. We're told we're not good enough our entire lives, and then we're supposed to know, with absolute certainty, that we are, despite years of mounting evidence, *deserving* of success.

That's not a syndrome within us. It's a natural reaction to societal cues about our ability.

I heard the brilliant software developer, Naomi Ceder, speak on this topic years ago, and it was perhaps the most impactful talk I've ever seen. Ever since, I cringe every time I hear a woman speak with shame about imposter syndrome. I don't like that women are taking the blame for having listened to a lifetime of societal cues. So-called imposter syndrome crops up only when women are finally stepping into their own and getting recognized for being brilliant and capable.

What Should We Be Doing?

Let's stop implying that the problem is internal to women, and instead focus on building one another up. We have some work to do, because we've heard and felt that we're not good enough for a long time.

In my circle of friends, I'm known for giving one heck of a pep talk. Were you fired? Going through a divorce?

Wondering why your children are so darn mean? I'm not the one you go to for wine and commiseration. No, I lack both time and patience for that kind of friendship.

But if you're looking for the kind of pep talk that will show you that your inner monologue is spinning lies and you are the undisputed worldwide champion of awesome, I'm your gal. Do you need someone who's been secretly collecting evidence of your accomplishments in order to bring them up exactly now, when you *most* need to be reminded? That's me.

And I learned everything I know from my husband.

I opened my talk at TEDxNormal on the pep talks my husband gives me. He said, "Get up there, peanut." He meant, "Go for it, hot stuff." Or sometimes he meant, "Go for the gold, sex machine." He says "Get up there, peanut!" when I need to be reminded to forge ahead, do the tough stuff, and take a risk. I think it's so beautiful. The rest of the talk focuses mostly on how incredibly good-looking he is, but I'll let you watch for yourself.

He told me once, "You don't get to decide if you're a loser or not. The rest of us already voted."

I had just been fired—unceremoniously and over the phone while I was shopping at Walmart. I had to sit down in the shoe section.

I hung up the phone, got up from the floor of the shoe section, hopped in the car, and ugly cried. I had ignored some pretty glaring red flags to take that job. The girlfriend who referred me in called me on the sly to tell me that the company culture was "awful—but you're an adult." I'm not an idiot, so I knew my time was limited, but still, nothing can make you feel more like a gigantic loser than getting fired.

For a few days, I wallowed in self-pity. I wondered aloud if I'd ever get a job again. Worse, I knew I was supposed to be *better* than that place. How did *they* fire *me?*

Like the gorgeous sunbeam of hope that he is, my husband said, "You don't get to decide.

"The world got together and voted, and we decided that you're awesome. And we aren't interested in your opinion. Not that you get a vote, but if you did, it would still be you against everyone else, so it wouldn't matter anyway. You're not a loser."

You might think you're a deadbeat. You might feel like an overgrown, awkward teenager who faked her way through. But I promise it's not up to you. We voted, and you're a winner. You're the Olympic gold medalist of fantastic and the mayor of Success Town.

It's hard to go after your dream job over and over again. It's hard to be told "no" over and over again. But when you finally get there and don't immediately feel you deserve to be there, it's not a syndrome that's internal to you.

It's the perfectly logical conclusion to a lifetime's worth of evidence.

But that's ok. This is an emperor-has-no-clothes situation: now that we've spoken the truth out loud, we can laugh about it and move on.

3 Steps to Stop Imposter Syndrome

See it for what it is. It's a lie. It's a clever way of arranging experiences to make it seem like you don't deserve the success you've earned.

Don't fall for it. There is a mountain of evidence that proves what a brilliant powerhouse you really are. Give that evidence weight.

Call it out for other people. Don't let another brilliant human sit with either the fear that they're an imposter or that their fear is a personal failing.

Join the conversation.

What pep talk would you give your younger self? What could you accomplish if you ignored nasty self-talk and listened to your biggest fans instead?

Post your response on Linkedin, tag me (Ashley Quinto Powell), and use the hashtag #executivemotherhood.

Why is it so hard to pay women?

I help women think through pay and self-advocacy all the time.

I spent years in staffing, so I've seen pay negotiations happen from every angle. I've spent even more years in sales, so I know all about pricing and closing.

But perhaps most importantly, when I have to advocate for myself, my natural inclination is to get emotional and start crying. It's mortifying. Nothing yells "I'm your most valuable employee!" like trying to subtly wipe both tears and snot away.

So if you think I'm a natural negotiator who just really knows how to get in there and demand what she wants, I promise it was lots of research, trial-and-error, and mentoring that made me knowledgeable and confident.

I will also credit my mother. She's a brilliant businesswoman but, more importantly, she has absolute blind faith in my abilities. Everyone needs a woman like her in their corner. She believes I should run every organization I've ever been a part of. She's always making suggestions like, "Ask for double what they offered!" or "See if you can have a company car!" or "See if they'll give you 50% equity!"

There's a pervasive myth that women don't get raises and promotions because they don't speak up. All they have to do is ask. So simple!

If only we had managed to ask for it, we would have been given equal pay long ago.

I'll pause for your eyeroll. For me, this is right up there with 'Be so good they can't tell you no,' which is also overly simplistic, terrible advice. (Let's be good at what we do and expect to be rewarded equally. The idea of being twice as good for the same reward makes me very, very tired.)

It's also okay if you're still in the camp that believes we just have to ask. I was there for many years, even as I taught people how to ask for more money. It's a convenient way to stay sane and take control of what you can.

The *Harvard Business Review* debunked this myth several years ago. A 2018 study showed we ask for raises as often as men but are less likely to get them.

We're asking. We just aren't getting the money.

We are trying to fight systemic problems at the individual level, which absolutely carries merit, but it's not the whole problem, and it's not the whole truth.

The whole truth is probably something closer to, "Girlfriend, you have to get really good at asking for more money because statistically you're at a disadvantage and you need to do everything you can to level the playing field—not just for yourself, but for others." That might not be the pep talk you were hoping for, but it has the advantage of being accurate.

Let's focus on what we *can* control: There is an art to asking for more, knowing what you're worth, and sticking to it. It starts with knowing, with absolute certainty, that you deserve big money.

Unfortunately, the vast majority of us have some money issues to work through before we can really think clearly about what we're worth.

If I distill down what I hear women express most around the topic of money and self-advocacy, I find three major hurdles:

- I don't think I'm worth it.
- I don't understand my worth.
- I don't need all that money.

To some extent, they're equally limiting, and I'll bet that one of these challenges is holding you back, too.

I don't think I'm worth it.

There's been enough written about confidence and self-worth for women, so I won't dwell on it here. But if you were in front of me today and told me you didn't think you were worth big money, I'd look at you as if you'd grown a horn.

Aren't you amazing at what you do? Aren't you putting care and attention and blood, sweat, and tears into everything you do? You should only have to be *as* good as the dudebro sitting next to you and you *know* you're harder-working, smarter, more delightful, and frankly, much better-looking. Friend, that dudebro is very busy convincing everyone that he's worth double what you are. Don't you dare let him get away with it. Get up there, peanut.

I don't understand my worth.

Without a doubt, you need to understand what you should be making. An internet search can help you pinpoint salaries adjusted for your level of experience and geographical area. That's easy.

The larger problem is that we don't understand *what's possible.* There isn't a class in high school that teaches you that you can carve out a bizarrely small niche for yourself, make buckets of money, and do work you love that no one has ever dreamed of—but there should be.

I grew up in downtown Chicago and my husband grew up in a small town in Wisconsin. There are some very obvious differences in our mindsets, the most interesting of which is how we think about our careers.

When my husband is thinking of what career he'd like to pursue, he looks around. He literally *looks around* and considers jobs he can see. He can see police officers, firefighters, teachers, doctors, and nurses. Going through an airport, he'll muse about being a flight attendant or a baggage handler. Everything in his consideration set is something he can lay eyes on.

I grew up in an eccentric apartment building in downtown Chicago that could have been the setting for the next *Tales of the City.* We had a neighbor who owned a company specializing in 900 numbers. I'm sure it was mostly phone sex hotlines and psychics, but he also owned a number that had a Spanish-speaking Santa line for kids to read off their Christmas lists. We loved to call and hear, "Ho, ho, ho, me llamo Santa!"

One of our neighbors was a well-known novelist who wrote screenplays for movie studios. Part of his business strategy was to sell scripts that never got made into movies—they were purchased so other movie studios couldn't buy them, but it meant a paycheck for him either way. Another neighbor ran a small airline. I grew up knowing music producers, advertising execs, commodities traders, hedge fund managers, and party planners. I knew that the world had as many niches as there were people.

I didn't see my career prospects as a handful of jobs I could pick from. I understood it was more dynamic than that.

But even recognizing the breadth of what I can do doesn't mean I fully understand *what's actually possible*.

As part of a speed-networking event, I was paired with a brilliant lawyer who offers legal services on a subscription model. To open the conversation, he asked me what goal I was working on, and I proudly replied,

"My goal is to make $250,000 while working 30 hours a week so I can spend more time with my kids."

Without blinking he said, "Is that a month?"

I had never been asked such a ridiculous question. A month? Of course not. *Who is this guy?*

Later, I shared this story with a small group of peers, expecting everyone to have the same reaction. To my surprise, the discussion wasn't about how out-of-touch and callous the lawyer had been. Rather, it became a discussion about whether $250,000 was livable in the midwest.

Liveable.

Sister, if you are thinking this is going to be a lesson in privilege or a commentary on the world's most callous and out-of-touch humans, I'm excited to say you are mistaken.

This is a lesson in thinking big.

My goal of $250,000 was plucked basically out of thin air. Someone I really admire made that salary in the 1990s and it sounded big to me. I had a goal to make six figures, and after I hit on that, I just picked $250,000 as a good next place to go.

But Henri Bendell as my witness, it never occurred to me to think bigger. And here I was, surrounded by peers who are in the same line of business, hustling the same hustle, wondering aloud if my Big Hairy Audacious Goal was *livable.*

That's hardly being audacious. It's hardly big, or hairy. (It's small and bald!) But how was I to know what my goal should be without first understanding what's possible?

It can feel like all the men got pulled into a room for a meeting where they learned how to negotiate, how much money they should make, and how to use the phrase, "Well, actually" to undermine coworkers. (It was probably right before they voted to make movies where chubby men marry models and chubby women are undateable.)

It can feel like there was a meeting we women all missed, but (well, actually) it was a hundred small meetings that we didn't even get invited to. I'm here to change that, so buckle up. This is the meeting.

> We don't know how to think *big* because we don't have a good definition of what *big* really is.

I shared this story about the lawyer and the $250,000-a-month with two women I really adore and admire.

Both are fabulously successful, self-made businesswomen. The first woman, who runs a large, well-known nonprofit, was right there with me in shock and indignation.

She said, "It's so weird. I am finally making $75,000 and it feels like such big money to me."

The other woman smiled a tight-lipped smile that made me *know* that six-figures-a-month is standard for her.

We need to talk more candidly about our money goals, especially if they're big. Yes. You heard me right. Talk OUT LOUD about your money goals. And if you don't have someone currently to talk with, hire a coach, or get different friends.

The last time I ran into my friend at the non-profit, she reported that she'd successfully campaigned for a big raise and had developed a plan to get to six figures with the next fiscal-year budget. Our money conversation created a spark that added nearly $10,000 to her income almost immediately, and she wouldn't have known it was a possibility otherwise.

You should be dreaming so much bigger than you are today. But until you understand that you have permission to think big, and until you then know what "big" really means, you're only speculating about what might be possible. And historically, we're not very good at knowing what the brass ring really looks like.

Start having more candid conversations about money with people you admire and trust. Join a coaching circle of incredibly successful people... but be careful.

If your goals are *really* big enough, there will be more than a handful of people who try to cut you down because of how your naked ambition makes them feel.

You'll never make that much money.

That's really unrealistic, don't you think?

Someone like you is never going to make it that big.

When are you going to get serious and get a real job?

Your success is very, very threatening. Do you have a plan for what happens the first time you make more money than your dad? When your income leapfrogs your spouse's?

A dynamic shift in any relationship is hard to weather, especially if you've always been the little girl who needs advice and encouragement. No one's expecting Tiny Tim to hit the gym and become a pro athlete. It's really comfortable to stay in the patterns we're used to.

You have enough problems fighting your own self-sabotage. You don't need anyone else's garbage thoughts taking up space.

I don't need all that money.

The most insidious and tricky mindset challenge is the idea that you come from humble beginnings, you're comfortable where you are, and you don't need all that money.

It's a cop-out.

I will occasionally say to a client, "You should be at double the rate you're at now." This is because we pervasively undervalue ourselves, whether we own our own business or bring home a salary. And where you might expect folks to say, "Fantastic! How do I get there?" they'll instead start listing off all the reasons they don't need more money.

> My husband makes plenty of money. I grew up in a family without much money and I've already come so far. If my bills are paid, I'm a happy woman. I'm really comfortable with where I am and what I'm doing and I just don't need a big salary and a stressful job.

If this is you, I'm going to call you out on this nonsense.

No one gives a flying fur coat about what you need. That's not the discussion you're *ever* having with an employer or a client. They don't care if your car is paid off or not, whether you rent or own, whether you have kids. Clients and employers care *only* about whether you are the best person for the job. Whether you pull up to the office in a brand new convertible or a busted minivan, no one is judging your budget.

No, it's not a budget discussion. It's a *worth* discussion. And if you're patting yourself on the back for being so darn humble and modest, you're a giant chicken. You don't want to ask for more because you're afraid someone will tell you "no" or think less of you for asking.

I have a rule that you can call me the B-word for $10,000.

If I ask for more money and you think to yourself, "What a witch!" (Of course, you didn't say witch. You said witch with a capital B), and you *still* pay me $10,000 more than you otherwise would, we're even. I'll even throw in "not a team player" for free.

And the opposite is also true.

If you're making the decision *not* to ask, you're the one paying $10,000 so someone doesn't call you a witch. Is it really worth it? You would never give a stranger money so they didn't mutter something mean about you under their breath. But in a negotiation, that's exactly the exchange we're making if we let ourselves off the hook because we're afraid of what someone will think of us for asking.

Nope, I don't care where you came from or what your budget needs are. It's the principle. You should be paid what you're worth *just because* you're worth it.

Don't worry about what you might need the money for; you'll figure that out later when you buy a car, take a vacation, or build generational wealth.

Sometimes I hear, "I don't need all that money; I would rather work for good people."

I don't want to work in a job I hate, at a corporation where I'm a cog in a wheel and don't get to spend any time with my family.

Why do we think we have to pick between making big bucks by working for the devil or making small potatoes by working for people who respect us?

It's nonsense. Where is the rule that makes us think good people don't have the money to pay us fairly? And what makes us think the dark side pays so well?

This line of thinking is a trap that keeps us where we are and convinces us to be happy with less than we deserve. If you haven't found the great values-driven, culture-forward work that pays well, keep looking. The best CEOs I've met wouldn't dream of underpaying you.

One such CEO is Amanda Moriuchi, the CEO of Appit Ventures, a rapidly growing, super successful software development firm. She competes for tech talent with the biggest, best-funded tech companies in the world, and wins every time.

Amanda did the research to understand what the median salary was for the metro area, broken down by years of experience, and put all the data into a big spreadsheet. When she interviews someone, she shows them the spreadsheet. She points out where they are on the X-axis for job junction and the Y-axis for years of experience, and says, "That's your salary. Next year, when you have another year of experience, you'll get a raise that will bump you up to the next number over. Does that work for you?"

She doesn't negotiate with anyone and she's transparent with everyone.

If the salary isn't appealing, she shakes the candidate's hand and wishes them luck. But mostly, candidates are grateful to know they're being treated fairly and equitably.

As I write this, we're experiencing the tightest market for senior tech talent in history. Developers are being offered 30% above their current salaries to jump ship. I had a client who, faced with having to replace three of his senior-most developers, decided to throw in the towel and close the company.

But that doesn't happen to Amanda. Her employees are grateful to know that they're being paid what they should be in a completely transparent way.

Not too long ago, I shared Amanda's story with my father, who'd had a successful executive career. He was baffled. "Why would anyone be ok with that? Don't they want to try for more?"

The thing about my dad is, he *knows* he'll come out ahead in a negotiation. The rest of us don't.

When I negotiate with my own incoming employees, I'm transparent from the start. Taking a page from Amanda, I pay everyone the same, and I'm transparent about the pay rate at every interaction, from the job description through the interviews. I want everyone who works with me to know, without a doubt, that I'm paying them the highest rate I can.

As women advance up the executive ranks, paying other women within those ranks fairly should be a top priority. That may mean salary overhauls for the entire company or making sure the women reporting to you make the same as the men reporting to you. I hope you'll make this a priority because, girlfriend, you are going big places and it would be a shame if you didn't change the world on your way.

As you're advocating for your own salary increases, the most critical piece is that you get over the fear of asking in the first place. "What do I do if they say 'no'?"

If they say "no," you have a choice—a well-informed choice, with no question that you could have gotten more or fared better. Many organizations are limited by their budget and will never be able to offer you more. If you love the work and can go in, eyes-wide-open about the money, you're still at an advantage. But more powerfully, you can say "no" right back. It's okay to walk away from an opportunity because it doesn't meet your salary requirements. As much as you may be completely in love with and born for a job, you can never really tell, from the outset, what it's going to be like once you accept the offer—but you can tell if the offer itself is any good.

The most disappointed I've ever felt about not getting a job was with The Mom Project—an amazing recruiting organization that specializes in helping working mothers advance their careers. I had been admiring them from afar for years and couldn't believe my luck when a recruiter reached out to me. They were looking for a Chief Revenue Officer who could take their company to the next level. They wanted candidates who could do public speaking on their behalf. (That's me!) And they were looking for someone with experience in staffing and recruiting sales. (Hello, more than a decade.) They were looking for someone passionate about working mothers. (Um, this book didn't exist *yet* but my TEDx on the subject certainly did.)

I was born for this role.

Except, I wasn't. They politely declined my enthusiastic candidacy.

And hired Serena Williams.

I'm not saying I lost the job to Serena Williams, but that's not *not* what I'm saying, either. She was hired for a very similar role and the CRO position wasn't filled. I'll let you do the math.

If I had to choose between myself and *Serena Williams* for a role, I'd pick Serena Williams, too.

That's the funny thing: they likely ended up offering her way more than they would have offered me. It wasn't about the money. It was about finding the best talent they possibly could.

I happened to be able to see who they hired. I mean, Bravo, folks. But you may never be able to see the truly stellar candidate who beat you for the job, or know how much they offered that candidate. And, more to the point, you may never know that the company with the perfect role that can't pay you what you're worth wasn't a perfect fit, after all. In fact, if they were really perfect, they'd pony up with a great offer.

They don't have to say, "Yes," but you do have to ask.

Years ago, I was managing a sales team of 10 at a big corporation. Every year, two members of that team would book a meeting to tell me how drastically I was underpaying them. The first guy I couldn't stand. He undermined me at every turn. He was difficult to work with, and, frankly, his work was just good enough *not* to get fired, but no better. The other guy was a star player and a dear friend. He was great at his job and fun to work with.

So, who got the raise?

That's a trick question. They both did! They were the only two people on the team who put me on notice that I was underpaying them. When it came time to advocate for raises on my team, I knew I had to take care of both of them. Looking back, I'm sure there were folks on that team who were silently stewing about their salaries. Had they said *anything*, I would have advocated harder on their behalf.

You are worth big money.

If it's time to put on your big-girl underpants and ask for a pay increase, consider this your sign. You can't settle for less. You know you're amazing. You know you have a stellar work ethic or a bonkers skill set or some unique expertise. Honoring those gifts means demanding that other people value them, too. Your children and the other women who look up to and admire you need to see that your enormous talent has great monetary value. Their talent does too. Bottom line?

Do not let fear diminish your trajectory. You were made for more.

Go get 'em, Tiger.

Join the conversation.

How are you addressing pay equity in your organization and for yourself?

Post your response on Linkedin, tag me (Ashley Quinto Powell), and use the hashtag #executivemotherhood.

In Pursuit of the Trophy for
Mom of the Year

There was a very specific moment in adulthood when I realized that I *could* be a parent.

I was 24. I'd just bought the world's cutest apartment in Wrigleyville in Chicago. I had a stable job I loved. I wasn't truly ready to be a parent. I didn't know my gorgeous lumberjack husband yet. I didn't really want to have kids. I just knew that if I *happened* to get pregnant, it wouldn't ruin my life. That doesn't sound like much, but for someone who only ever considered how a pregnancy would derail all her plans, it was a pretty big deal.

With surprising frequency, a young woman without kids will attend one of my talks or webinars and tell me they want to have children but can't see how that would ever fit into their lifestyle. They're upwardly mobile, dedicated to their careers, and thinking that if they *happened* to get pregnant, it wouldn't be the worst thing in the world, but it wouldn't be great, either. They can't see how they'd be able to keep their career on track and raise a child. Why? Because they don't have many examples of young mothers who aren't being gently shamed into leaving their ambitions behind.

Children are amazing. Even though my pregnancies were mostly miserable, I loved being pregnant. I loved feeling my body change, and the baby kick. That's saying a lot because I did my best to make pregnancy unappealing to anyone paying attention.

I ate every burrito in a three-mile radius and was still hungry. All the time. My stomach would growl *as I was eating.*

I was so bloated that my poor toes looked like they were going to pop off my feet. At my doctor's office, the nurses would tip their heads to the side and furrow their brows with sympathy—and then scramble to take my blood pressure, sure I had preeclampsia and always genuinely surprised when I didn't.

I had obscure pregnancy symptoms that no one warned me about. Pregnancy-induced Carpal Tunnel Syndrome. Frequent nose bleeds. Acid reflux. Did you know that babies in utero get hiccups? They love to stretch out with their feet in your ribs and push hard enough that you expect to deliver a small CrossFit athlete who never missed leg day. I slept so lightly that my breath turning bad would wake me up.

The only thing that couldn't wake me was my own snoring. I snored so loudly that my husband made a recording of it so he could prove how awful it was. It wasn't one of his finer moments. Instead of calmly acknowledging that he was right about my snoring, I burst into a hysterical sobbing fit. (That recording still lives on his phone and will occasionally make its way into a playlist so we can revisit how insensitive it is to make a recording of your wife. Who is pregnant with your child. And very miserable. And can't do anything about the snoring. *And WHY did you have to embarrass me?*)

And I was the size of a majestic sea mammal. Without exaggeration, I was a walking Orca who needed to be returned to sea because it was too difficult to breathe without floating in buoyant water. In my winter pregnancy, no coat available to the general public would fit me, so I had to wear a full-length mink coat. That sounds glamorous as I write it here, but please trust me. I looked like Hagrid. I'm confident that everyone who saw me walking heard a tuba toot with every step.

This would have been a great opportunity to address high school students. *Use condoms, kids. Because if you don't, you could end up looking like* this.

But no matter how terrible pregnancy is, and it can be pretty awful, you are still ground zero for a miracle.

Raising children allows you to heal and repair your own childhood. You understand your own parents more and blame them less. You get a chance to raise your children the way you wish you were raised. You either gain understanding about why your parents weren't at all your soccer games or commit to being at every game your kid ever plays. Sometimes both.

I was raised in a family that wasn't very active. I have a brother with special needs and substantial mobility issues, so instead of vacations to state parks, we went to fancy restaurants all over the world. We spent one summer in an apartment in Rome, another summer at an apartment in southern Spain. To be clear, I have no complaints. It was a truly incredible privilege to be raised that way. But for my own family, I wanted to be active the way my friends' families were.

I was an adult when I learned how life-affirming it is to be in nature. I want my children to know how great it feels to be active in the outdoors, so despite their frequent protests, we go on outdoor adventures quite a lot. I'm certain that when they have kids, they'll joke about how I raised them like feral wolves and raise their children like the bourgeoisie.

My daughter is gorgeous. I can spend hours watching her expressive features and the beautiful way she moves her body through space.

I remember having that body as a little girl, but I didn't think it was beautiful when I had it. When it was my body, it was chubby and slow, and uncooperative. When I watch my daughter, I'm overcome both by my intense appreciation of her beauty and an acknowledgment of my own. I wasn't loved *despite* being a chubby kid. My parents loved me and thought I was marvelous without the qualifiers I always assumed were there.

My parents didn't think I was cute *even though* I was chubby. They thought I was cute. They didn't delight in my little fingers and toes and *ignore* my baby fat. They delighted in my fingers and toes and everything else about me.

The experience of watching and adoring my daughter helped me revisit old memories with a new perspective and see how wonderful and beautiful I was—*and still am!*

As a parent, it's dazzling to experience your own childhood through this lens. You better understand the circumstances your parents dealt with because those circumstances are repeated. This time, you get to be the parent. You get to reconsider the stories of your childhood with an understanding of the whole equation.

I'm quick to joke about the trials and tribulations of being a mom, but it's honestly make-your-heart-explode phenomenal. It's not in everyone's plan, but if it's in yours, it's pretty great.

I tend to make a distinction between working motherhood and *executive motherhood.*

Some moms work in a way that prioritizes their home life. They've built their careers to make space for a family. They might take time off to raise kids and not be concerned one bit about the impact on their lifetime earning potential.

Then there are folks like me.

We thrive at work. We're ambitious. We expect our talents to make a big impact on the world. We want to be the CEO. We want to create seven-figure businesses.

We haven't chosen our profession because it allows for work-life balance. Oh no. We chose our roles because they ignited a fire in us. For better or for worse, our professional goals are a big part of our identity.

Sue Marks is the legendary founder and CEO of Cielo Talent. They have offices all over the world and estimated annual revenue well above two hundred million. I once heard her say, "Business *is* personal."

Sure, it's not terribly healthy to align your identity with a company and a specific role. But being an ambitious, accomplished person who thinks deeply about how you're impacting the world is different. It isn't a hat you can take off when you walk through the door. You go home thinking about clients and projects. While you're feeding the baby, you're coming up with ways to remove the roadblocks between you and your professional goals. You love the work you do.

Years ago, I created a group of career-driven, butt-kicking, powerhouse moms. It grew quickly and I ended up giving my TEDx about why we needed that community. (Well, that topic was very secondary to the larger subject, "How hot is my husband, am I right?")

In my talk, I made the point that we assume all moms want to talk exclusively about coupons and recipes and the best organizational tools for a minivan. Instead of trying to keep a mom in the workforce, we assume she's going to leave, and subtly push her out. We need to create a culture that supports and encourages women to thrive at work in those first few incredibly difficult years of motherhood so we can preserve our pipeline of executive women.

Post-pandemic, it's even more critical.

I frequently get asked, "How do you do it all?"

I'm not special. Every woman with a visibly successful career gets asked this question three times a week. It's annoying and clichéd. There must be a top-secret guide about how to talk to women that insists this question be asked within the first seven minutes.

But when I am asked, "Ashley, how do you do it all? How do you have those gorgeous, well-behaved children and that incredibly handsome husband and a straight-up business empire?" I always answer it.

In fairness, I've only been asked that *exact* question once or twice.

But I answer it in one of three ways:

1. I have plenty of help.
2. I'm exhausted but it's worth it.
3. I'm an idiot.

They're all true.

I *do* have incredible help from family and neighbors and an entire team of virtual assistants. I *am* tired but I have an amazing life and an important mission. As my father says, you can sleep when you're dead.

And yes, I am absolutely, without question, an idiot. I get excited about projects and dive in, head first, even if my plate is already overflowing. If there is a plea from the girl scouts for a troop leader or a committee that needs me, I say "Yes!" like I have no short-term memory.

It's important to answer the question, "How do you do it all?" in whatever way feels authentic to you and to the moment, because other women are watching. Men might ask because they've run out of conversation topics. But women are listening to hear how we do it, so they can do it, too.

There are great roadmaps for women who want to dial back their careers while they raise kids. But if you want to stay in the game, keep your career pointed way up and to the right, and continue your journey to the top, you don't have readily available tools or advice.

Women listening for this advice want to hear, very specifically, what works for you so they can piece together what works for them. Some of that advice can be hard to say aloud and hard to hear. It's different from the techniques that work for stay-at-home moms.

My mother gave me the advice *not* to call my kids while I was traveling. It was hard advice to hear. I had a strict policy that if I wasn't in town to tuck my kids in at night, I would at least call them at bedtime.

As a rule, I remember that my own mother hung the moon.

She had an incredible career as an executive and as an entrepreneur. She has great business acumen. She's gutsy and brave.

But her advice stung. The kids did not need to know I was there for them. I wasn't. My bedtime calls made *me* feel better, but it reminded my kids that they were missing out and re-opened a wound every time.

Her advice stung, but she was right.

(Please, for the love of Betsy Johnson, do not tell her. I beg you. She has a long memory and an unfortunate habit of remembering times when she was right 30 years ago as if they were yesterday. My father once told her to wait to buy a purse in Hong Kong because she'd probably see it elsewhere for less. She didn't. It still gets brought up three times a year which is really saying something because it happened in 1992.)

To streamline their morning routine, one woman told me privately that she dresses her kids the night before and has them sleep in their clothes. It's a brilliant idea, but no one wants to admit that they shortcut pajamas.

I regularly use a virtual assistant to step in on kid stuff. VAs do the planning for my girl scout meetings. They pick the craft, the songs, and the videos. A VA makes sure boy scout activities are in my calendar. I rely on my VA's professional assistance with *everything* I need to get done—not just the strictly professional stuff. It works well, but no one wants to admit that they outsource any part of parenting.

We don't like hearing this type of advice because it runs contrary to what we've been taught a mother *should* be. A mother should be loving and caring and warm. She makes nutritious meals and sings lullabies and cheers from the sidelines of all the soccer games.

That model is based on the talents and experiences of a stay-at-home mom. We don't consider that a mother *should* be modeling how to be a successful person, how to advocate for her own needs, or how to create a life of joy when the world isn't built for her.

We don't do well when we try to recreate the experiences of a stay-at-home mom. We'll never live up. We might never be the mom who bakes brownies for the class or spends time making elaborate bento lunch boxes. We might not have the capacity to coach our kids' sports teams or chaperone the school dance.

If we ignore the stay-at-home model, we can stop fixating on the things we're missing out on, and start to flex into the *advantages* of being a working mom.

We can advise our children into adulthood about everything from building a business to landing a job to the importance of networking. Because we have less *quantity* time, we can have more focused, meaningful *quality* time with our children. We have more resources in our connections, our wallets, and our frequent flyer miles.

If your career allows you to have a big impact on the world, to create opportunities for those around you, to lift as you rise, you make a *spectacular* role model for your children.

Our children are incredibly lucky to have front-row fashion-show seats as we navigate work-life balance and as we struggle and succeed.

Babe, you are a powerful example to your children exactly as you are. Your children will not look back at their childhoods and wish you'd dragged them along to the grocery store every Tuesday and hovered over their classrooms year after year. They won't care that you didn't actually bake cookies from scratch or make cutesy snacks.

They'll be proud to have had a powerhouse woman at the helm and will build on the example you've given them.

Your kids are really, really lucky to be your kids. Even if they won't tell you for 20 years.

Join the conversation.

How do *you* do it all? What are your best tips for other working moms?

Post your response on Linkedin, tag me (Ashley Quinto Powell), and use the hashtag #executivemotherhood.

Working Moms Do it Better

Lately, I've been scolding myself for taking naps.

To be fair, I nap almost every day, which is unusual for the over-five sets. Outwardly, I'm flippant and proud. *One of the advantages of being my own boss!*

But inwardly, my self-talk is vicious. *Why can't I make it through the day like everybody else? Is it medical? I should see a doctor. Maybe my body doesn't like when I eat carbs. Maybe I need to exercise more. I need better self-discipline; this is a character flaw. This is unattractive. My husband is going to see what a lazy lump I am. This is a symptom of being so fat. I need to lose weight to have more energy, and if I'd done that already, I wouldn't be taking naps now and I did this to myself. You know what, this is depression. It's seeping in because I didn't protect my mental health and now I have to get Sisyphus's boulder up the hill* again.

I can go on in this spiral for a long while, eventually scolding myself for not having deep enough relationships with my friends and family, not being able to delegate properly, run a business, be a mom…..

It wasn't until a few days ago that I had a grand realization. By way of justifying an afternoon nap I was just groggily waking up from, I told my husband that I had two speaking engagements today and that those always take a lot out of me.

Yes, speaking engagements *do* take it out of me. The rest of the day had been wall-to-wall 1:1 meetings where almost everyone said, "Wow! I love your energy!"

That's a compliment I love and get frequently. I've always known I get energy from interacting with powerhouse women, and I give it right back.

When I first started networking years ago, I used to come home practically dancing at the end of the day. I met the neatest person! They're doing amazing things! We're going to collaborate on something fantastic!

I'm not doing a 1:1 coffee or two a day anymore, I'm doing, without exaggerating, six or eight virtual coffees back-to-back (to-back-to-back).

I'm not complaining; that's how I do business. I have meetings to talk about my virtual assistant company, meetings to talk about the networking groups I run, and meetings to talk about my consulting services. All around those business development calls, I'll have networking calls, client coaching meetings, and team meetings.

I'm not complaining; I love it. Those interactions bring me heaps of joy, and even more if whoever I'm meeting with joins my networking groups, hires one of my virtual assistants, or brings me on as a consultant.

I'm not complaining; I'm just exhausted. I swear to Coco Chanel, it didn't occur to me that after seven hours of energy-intensive meetings that I *deserved* to be tired.

In this season of my life, I'm running three businesses and doing lots of public speaking. I'm trying to be active in my community, spend time with my children, and maintain a great relationship with my husband. An outsider might note that it would be awfully difficult to *also* cook a healthy dinner every night, make time for friends, and do any amount of self-care. And yet, here I am, scolding myself for being a gigantic, lazy failure.

I'm not unique. I'll bet you're over there scolding yourself for not being able to do everything. Maybe your body doesn't steal naps. Maybe your body craves alcohol or doesn't eat. And as you and I are stuck in a cycle of self-flagellation and guilt, we're getting plenty of messages that everyone else is doing (and being) more than we are.

During the pandemic, as I was trying to navigate simultaneously working from home and administering virtual school, I was also gaining a non-trivial amount of weight. (The COVID-19 19, am I right, ladies?) I hired a wellness coach who was really wonderful but didn't have the same pandemic challenges I did. Specifically, she was single with no kids.

During one of our sessions, I explained that I was really and truly more overwhelmed than I had ever been before. I wasn't successfully making time for exercise because my kids always needed me for something. I was trying to run my business in the stolen minutes during the day and after everyone went to bed. Context switching between client work and solving virtual classroom Zoom issues was giving me near-daily migraines. It wasn't pretty.

As I explained that I was defeated before the day began, she told me we needed to focus on my "why." *Focus on my why?* I like Simon Sinek as much as the next gal, but I did not need to focus on my why. I needed to focus on my *"how."* I *needed* childcare.

I didn't need to dig deep within and have a profound mindset shift. I needed a nanny and some antidepressants.

Society says this kind of nonsense to us all the time. Here we are again, searching for an *internal solution* to an *external problem*. You were probably in the same boat, frantically paddling your way through disproportionate childcare and household duties while pretending that everything was fine at a full-time job. You deserve an adult girl-scout badge just for surviving, even if you didn't survive completely intact.

And if anyone told you to enjoy this time with your family or asked what pandemic hobby you picked up, I hope you put salt in their morning coffee or a horse head in their bed.

We place immense pressure on ourselves (or it is placed on us) and the help we're offered often involves changing some crucial piece of *our* understanding, not tangible help.

I hate to hear women joke about needing a glass of wine at the end of the day, but I get it. When "mommy juice" and "mommy's sippy cup" become a meme, we should examine why so many moms are being driven to drink.

I'm not saying that moms should take it easy, or stop doing things that make them busy. I've been going at this pace since college and I have no intention of stopping.

There's some work I do that when I hustle, it's to make money for my family. I can't stop. I can't take it easy. Treat me like a marathon runner: make sure I have water and an energy bar every once in a while and cheer me on!

No, I'm not saying stop. If you're a dynamo, keep going. The world needs to see you. The world needs the amazing work you're doing. But let's figure out how to enable you to do that amazing work without piling on guilt about what you're *not* able to do.

Years ago, when I was traveling frequently for work and having a hard time being on the road, I always got advice about how to advocate for myself to travel less. With few exceptions, I was never given advice on how to manage travel better or how to stay connected with my family while I was on the road.

My father traveled frequently for business when I was a kid. He did business with clients in London, Dubai, Riyadh, and Tokyo, to name a few. I told my father about the immense guilt I felt being away and he looked at me horrified. "Why? That's your *job*. I never felt any guilt about being away. Why do you?"

It's different for moms, but it doesn't have to be. I was proud of my dad. I knew he was doing important things and I hoped that one day, I'd have a career like his.

We treat women and moms so differently.

My friend, Karen, met her husband while they were doing the exact same job for the exact same company. Once they had kids, she saw the stark contrast between how they were treated. If he left early to pick the kids up from school he was applauded as Dad of the Year. And if she left early for the same reason, she'd get an eye roll and an implied judgment on her ability to get her job done.

As we're doing important work around implicit bias, we need to make sure we're addressing the way we think of and treat moms at work.

It should be no surprise that if we build female leaders while they're young, then make it impossible to stay in the workforce exactly as they're gaining true expertise, that we won't have women in senior leadership.

I remember being called into my boss's office at about eight-months-pregnant and asked, "Are you coming back after maternity leave?" I was dumbfounded—I literally didn't understand the question.

She wanted me to be straight with her. Was I going to come back to work after being at home, or would I resign instead of returning?

Frankly, this seemed like the least likely scenario. I loved my job, where I was happy, successful, and upwardly mobile. I was the bigger breadwinner in my marriage. And I had never mentioned wanting to stay home. Not once.

This sort of cue about our belonging in the workforce is a prime contributor to the decision to be a stay-at-home mom.

Imagine (or remember) you're in those first couple years of motherhood, where you're a giant leaky boob and everything's difficult. If your partner says, "Gee, what if you took a few years and stayed home?" and you take them up on it, you'll be giving your partner's career a boost in exchange for your own.

We tend to think that stay-at-home moms are being supported by their spouses. It's certainly a wonderful privilege, but any stay-at-home parent will tell you it's hard work. It might not come with a paycheck, but having a partner who takes care of everything at home boosts a working spouse's career prospects. A family's income can often be larger with one parent working than if both parents work because the worker-bee can have a singular focus. The worker-bee can drive their career forward, unfettered by concerns about family finances, dinners, grocery shopping, and laundry. Corporate types call that drive and singular focus *management potential*.

While my husband stayed home, we knew that we were sacrificing his career for the sake of mine. It's an okay decision to make, and I'm glad we made it.

We can't let working spouses peacock around believing their income is bigger solely because of their own talent, and not because of the enormous amount of help they have on the homefront.

If you *do* have a spouse that stays at home, no matter their gender, you should always remember to do the following:

> When you walk in the door, immediately start being helpful. Don't you dare talk about how tired you are or how difficult your day was. Unless you accidentally blocked the Suez Canal with a supercargo ship or were the one to unblock it, you don't have a leg to stand on.
>
> Tell everyone how hard your spouse works and how difficult it must be to stay at home. Talk about it at neighborhood picnics, family birthday parties, and

anytime you mention your own work. I promise, your job is not more stressful than cleaning up the third diaper blowout today while a tiny dictator screams and throws Duplos.

Never, ever mention that the house is a mess, that laundry isn't done, or that dinner isn't perfect. Order a pizza, vacuum the living room, and remind your spouse how good-looking they are in sweatpants.

I prefer to be the working parent, but sometimes it's tempting to think the grass is greener. A colleague of mine once expressed guilt about not being at home for her children, thinking of all the quality time they'd spend together.

She was envisioning that they'd be skipping hand-in-hand to a playground where she'd push kiddos on the swing and catch them as they came down the slide.

"No," I told her. "You'd be grocery shopping and folding underpants."

Being a stay-at-home parent isn't glamorous, but societal expectation tells us we'd be Mary Poppins if we didn't work, and guilt tells us we need to make up for our absence. We rarely, if ever, hear a woman talk bluntly about what she's *not* doing or has consciously taken off her plate. Instead, there's an implication that she's trying to have it all and do it all—and if she's succeeding at one, we assume she's failing at the other.

We have inherited some false beliefs about working mothers around productivity, contribution, and dedication. Our biases make us believe that mothers at work have less to offer, but the opposite is true. With more on her plate, a successful working mother is the embodiment of the phrase, "busy people get more done." She's a more empathetic manager and a time management wizard. She has more at stake and holds more responsibility as the head of a household than she ever did before kids.

That's good news for a growing company.

Think of a company that started as a scrappy startup and is on its way to being a unicorn with a billion-dollar valuation. As a startup, the company will likely attract and employ young people who are happy to work long hours, wear lots of hats, and push the company from viable to thriving. In the early stages, those employees won't care terribly about benefits and stability. But when they start getting married and thinking about having children, the instability of a startup isn't going to fly. Those employees will leave for stable jobs at stable companies.

Once our scrappy startup starts to gain traction, employees will feel the company becoming more stable and they'll be able to see a future for the company—and for themselves within it.

> We should look at our employees' growing families as evidence of success.

In the work I do with companies to build great sales engines, I get really excited when the company starts to see its employees buy houses, get married, and have babies. It shows that employees are confident in a company's ability to generate revenue long enough into the future that they feel safe putting down roots. It's a powerful index because if you're doing it correctly, the economic impact is incredibly far-reaching.

A business owner can create a foundation for amazing growth, evidenced by marriages and tiny humans. But my love of the marriage-baby index is unique. As teams start to mature, leadership tends to view pregnant women as less dedicated and productive—not more.

Women are in a difficult position. When their expertise matures, they're ready for their personal lives to follow suit. But when women are ready for kids, they're also keenly aware that pregnancy and children will hurt their career prospects.

I'm consistently surprised that when I speak about being a working mother and how I do (or do not) make it all work, the women who want to speak with me afterward aren't moms. They're women who want to have kids but don't see any way to fit that goal into their current career and lifestyle.

As much as I would like to change the world by sharing the statistics, the only way to really create change is to have *fathers* take parental leave with the same frequency that women do.

If men took substantial leave when they had children, it wouldn't be considered a women's issue. It would be a *human* issue. (It's much the same as the age-old joke: if men had periods we would have solved PMS a long time ago.)

Companies creating space for parental absences would be more common and we'd get used to having new parents take the time they need. As a bonus, we could stop fawning over the office Dads who get outsized credit for doing completely standard parenting things.

When I was pregnant with my second baby, my husband worked out a whopping three half-days of paternity leave.

Not three-and-a-half days. Three half-days.

And in the 12 hours he took to bond with his baby daughter, he spent most of it concerned that he would face consequences for taking even that much time.

It's true that we're not kind to women, but it's also true that we're not kind to parents, no matter the gender. If we fight for one thing, please let it be paternity leave. Much of our energy is focused on the fight for (and the fight by) women, but our partners are missing out in big ways, too.

And anyway, how surprised will they be that we're fighting this battle on their behalf?

Hopefully, surprised enough to fight for us in return.

Join the conversation.

Are you more productive now that you have kiddos? Who are your best male allies?

Post your response on Linkedin, tag me (Ashley Quinto Powell), and use the hashtag #executivemotherhood.

Change starts with you, Friend.

A funny thing happens in schools. 75% of teachers are women, but nearly half of school principals are men. We usher those men *right to the top.*

When my husband went back to work, I joked that as a tall, white, bearded, handsome man, he was going to be promoted within the first month. As it happened, he was asked about and encouraged to pursue a management track within the first *week.*

Logically, we should know that a Y chromosome isn't the management potential gene, but we sure treat it like it is.

Statistically, women must be more educated, with more degrees and certifications, to get the same jobs. It's one of the reasons women carry fully two-thirds of the total student loan debt in the US.

This is especially true for women of color. For so long the narrative has been, "work so hard they can't tell you "no," and that's translated directly into "work twice as hard for a lower wage."

To explain the obvious absence of women in tech, there's a myth that says women are naturally really creative and just better at "soft skills"; *that's* why there aren't many women in high-paying, technical roles.

Well, maybe this isn't completely untrue—after all, we live up to our reputation as fantastic leaders with emotional intelligence through the roof. But we *also* have stellar technical skills. I can point to thousands of women in tech whose technical chops outperform those of their male counterparts.

But let's back up just a doggone minute. Why would anyone assume creativity and soft skills aren't useful in tech or business?

I contend I've been successful precisely *because* I'm creative.

It's all those years as a theater kid in the '90s that put me on stage today. Being creative in a general sense has led me to imagine, try, and complete innovative projects in web design and development. Heck, I got into development because the world needed an e-commerce site for gigantic costume jewelry.

This is a serious problem if you think about the way we defund arts education and devalue the humanities, but throw our energy and financial support into STEM. I'm aware that STEAM programs include art, but frankly, it's an afterthought. What about history? Literature? It's *all important*, especially as we're educating and encouraging our children.

Let me ask you a question. Did you have to change or hide a fundamental part of who you are to get where you are today?

If you answered "Yes," you are not alone. You're probably a successful, driven woman. Or, more likely than not, someone who's well on her way. Or maybe you are someone who loves successful, driven women, in which case, you have *great* taste. So the question then is:

Did you, or will you, have to replace any of your feminine qualities with masculine ones?

There is often an unspoken rule that women are stronger with soft skills and therefore better suited for less aggressive careers. The image of business being an old boys' club, with men in suits making hard-nosed business deals, is no accident. And while that image *should* be fairly old-timey now, it's still alive and well in tech and venture capital, where women get less than 2% of venture funding. If you look at the startup and venture capital space, the stakeholders are overwhelmingly young, white, and male. They might be mistaken for a college lacrosse team or Irish hurlers. (Look it up.)

I spent years telling myself and everyone else that I wasn't a competitive person. Actually, that's far from the truth. I just don't like sports. My career in sales has been successful in large part because I'm competitive and goal-oriented. Early in my career, I was the only woman on my team and consciously cultivated an aggressive, competitive style to keep up. There was an unspoken rule that women were better suited for the other, less aggressive teams. Sales was meant for the big boys.

I was proud to be tough enough to make it on a sales team. A colleague who watched me doggedly pursue and close a deal said, "Jesus, Ashley. You're a monster." He meant it as a compliment and I took it as one.

To everyone's credit, diversity has become a priority for any company that expects to still be in business in 10 years. Instead of a homogeneous group of people shaping the way business is conducted, the unspoken rules of the game are being influenced by a more diverse group of thinkers.

As more and more women move into senior leadership, we are fundamentally changing how business is done.

We don't have to settle for rules written by the boys. We can build businesses that benefit stakeholders at every level. We can foster environments where other women, especially mothers, succeed and grow.

We *must* protect our pipeline of executive women.

But as with any marginalized group, it's too much to ask working women to take on the burden of both *living* with underrepresentation, inequity, and bias, and *fixing* underrepresentation, inequity, and bias. It just can't be done. We need allies, and we need them everywhere.

We've got to have allies at home, from our spouses who tell us to "Get up there, peanut" to our little people who look up to us and cheer us on. And we have to have allies advocating for us at all levels of our organizations, with men who attend our women's ERG programming and higher-ups who sponsor and champion us.

I do LOVE femme-exclusive spaces, but I've learned so much from mentors and friends who've always asked,

"But where are the men? How are you going to get where you want to go without them?"

And the truth is, we can't. Men: We need you and your allyship more than ever.

We need you to step forward as supportive fathers and partners who don't just talk the talk. We need you to walk the walk—to daycare pickup and the grocery store. We need you to be okay taking time away from your work to be with your children, whether that's Tuesday and Thursday afternoons or the two years after the baby is born.

Men deserve the opportunity to parent and bond with their children at an early stage.

When a woman is on maternity leave, caring for her newborn, she's developing a routine. She's getting to know her baby and its cries. She knows how and when to get the baby down for a nap. She knows exactly what will happen if we lose the stuffed lamb, Carl, and she has learned the hard way that you must keep track of its whereabouts at all times because if Carl goes missing no one in this house will ever sleep.

Men who are at work through the early infant stages don't get the opportunity to learn the minutiae of the routine and will always seem to be the lesser parent.

It will appear to anyone paying attention that Mom knows what she's doing and Dad is a lovable doofus. And frankly, who could blame Dad for relying on his doofus status to get out of changing a diaper blowout?

And we bear some of the blame, too. Because it feels darn good to be the best parent in the room. It's fun to know exactly where that sneaky Carl gets hidden. It's amazing to be the one whose kiss can heal an injury or whose hug can make things better.

But if we don't share the early bonding and allow our partners to step in and step up, we'll never have help. We'll spend our days being the only one who knows how to put the baby down and we'll never be able to leave the house.

If I hadn't been ok with an orange living room, if I had really stuck to my guns and said, "This is my house and it will *not* have a color scheme like a tasteful circus," I couldn't have taken my dream job in Chicago.

We can't have it both ways.

But I know you, and I know what you're capable of. You are capable of big things. You deserve the chance to accomplish them.

And men, you deserve the opportunity to know your children and shape their lives. You deserve to have a deep connection with the incredible little people you created.

You've got this. I'm rooting for you.

Join the conversation.

How did your partner's family leave help shape the parents you both are today?

Post your response on Linkedin, tag me (Ashley Quinto Powell), and use the hashtag #executivemotherhood.

The Fix

I met Dorothy when I was going back and forth between Chicago and Madison. I was in the prime of my career, and *very* proud of my job and my Chicago pied-à-terre. She and I were connected by a friend who knew we both had big jobs and incredibly supportive husbands.

I liked this woman from the instant I met her. She had been a major player in her industry and had seen enormous success. Her husband had stayed at home with the kids, which allowed for her career to grow and thrive. Now that she was close to retirement, she was working on some passion projects.

Shortly after our first meeting, Dorothy invited me to breakfast but didn't order anything for herself.

"Listen," she said, as I dove headfirst into my eggs. "I have to tell you something really, really important."

She explained that her husband had been diagnosed with terminal cancer and they were looking back on their lives, wondering if they'd done the right thing.

Her career had been huge. She built a multi-million dollar company in the 1990s and early 2000s. At home, her husband did everything—the cooking, cleaning, and kid-chauffeuring—so she could concentrate on running and growing the business. He had a low-stress, part-time job that gave him a little something to do, but mostly he raised their kids and looked after the house.

It sounded like a dream to me—and it was for her. She was a big deal in a big city. A big fish in a big pond. She was confident everything and everyone was well cared-for at home while she brokered deals and hobnobbed with the city's most influential people.

What an amazing setup! It was everything I was trying to build.

Reflecting now, she wasn't so sure they *had* done the right thing.

He didn't have a chance to pursue his own aspirations. He was busy supporting their family as she pursued hers. Now that the end of his life was in sight, he wondered what he might have been capable of had he gotten the chance to spread his wings.

"I kept him small. So I could be big."

It struck a chord. It's a badge of honor to have a stay-at-home spouse. If you want to make sure everyone knows you're a big deal, nothing says "I make as much money as two people" like having a spouse stay at home.

My own ego adored the setup. But I love my husband fiercely. Was I keeping him small so I could be big?

I sat on this for weeks. I didn't know how to ask a question that big.

Were we doing it all wrong? Had I assumed that raising our family was enough for him, while he secretly harbored dreams of doing something else?

The previous year, I had given my husband a standup comedy class as a Christmas gift. At the time, Sean looked at me incredulously and said, "What would make you think I'd want to do *that*?"

He listens to stand-up comedy the way other people listen to music. He's hilarious. And he's a giant ham. After a month of telling me he wasn't taking the class and I should figure out how to get my money back, he relented.

He loved the class. And in the capstone performance, he slayed.

Maybe Sean wanted to pursue a comedy career. If he was giving me time, space, and support, I could certainly return the favor.

After ruminating on it for about a month, I told him the whole story of meeting Dorothy and her urgent warning.

"Listen, babe. If you want to do something else, let's figure out how to make it happen. If that's comedy, we have the Chicago apartment. We can trade places and I'll handle everything at home while you network and perform at comedy clubs on the weekends. I don't want you to wake up in 20 years regretting the way we've lived our lives."

He looked at me and said, "I've been thinking about something, too."

My breath caught in my throat.

"Are you going to regret missing out on so much at home? This is fun. The kids are growing up fast and they're not going to be this age forever."

I truly don't need to be home for the little stuff. My soul doesn't ache to give baths every night and make lunches every morning. I love the time I spend with my children. And I love being able to pursue my ambitions. I wasn't missing out.

My husband confessed that leaving every weekend wasn't appealing at all. He didn't want to push hard toward a big, hairy, audacious goal. His soul was right where it wanted to be.

The discussion was a worthy one. We had the opportunity to check in with one another and make sure we were building the life *both* of us wanted to lead.

I imagine stay-at-home moms have the same duality. Some are happy exactly where they are, present for all of the little stuff. And some are aching to see how far they could go if they had support and opportunity.

It's not important that every man light the world on fire with a big, impactful career. And it's not important that every woman be present for every single dinner, bath, and soccer game.

It's important that we have the option to be *where* we want to be *when* we want to be there.

Toots, the world needs you. It doesn't need a miserable, compromised version of you. It doesn't need the overworked, frazzled you that's trying to live up to unreasonable expectations. Or the dimmed, weary version who's afraid to dream.

The world needs the version of you with big, expansive goals. It needs you to step up as the Mayor of Successstown, the Titan of Modern Industry, the Wizard of Results.

Your children need it.

Other women need it.

The world needs it.

I know you can do it. Get up there, peanut.

I asked the smartest people I know this question: If you could wave a magic wand and change one thing for working parents (at home, work, or elsewhere), what would you change?

I got back some brilliant answers.

> "If I could wave a magic wand and change one thing for working parents at home and work it would be gender norms, hands down. We still expect women to earn a living and do most of the domestic work. In a household with two working parents, we expect mothers to still be primary caregivers; otherwise, we see them as "bad parents." That's bullshit. I know men right now who expect women to cook, clean, care for the children and earn a living, while they only put in

their eight hours of work. That's it. Again, that's bullshit."

Dr. Sagashus Levingston, CEO/Founder of
Infamous Mothers, LLC, Mom of six

"I'd change the cultural pressure to do it all. As a working mom, I constantly feel like I'm failing if I'm not firing on all cylinders in every area of my life. There is a cultural expectation that the kids come first and everything else comes after. And, while I love my children and would do anything for them, I need to come first sometimes to allow me to show up as my best self for my family and my coworkers later. We also need to celebrate and recognize those hard-working dads who hold down the fort in an untraditional manner. My husband does dishes and laundry, shuffles the kids to practice, and cooks dinner when I am at a work event on a weeknight. Our roles are outside of the cultural norm, but it's the only way it works right now. Ultimately, I want my boys to be raised in a household and a world where anyone can be successful and know that the definition of success varies for each of us. Their success should be defined by their own personal happiness and fulfillment."

Ami, Community Bank CFO, and Boy Mom

"Wives for everyone! If only I had a dollar for every time I have said I need a wife'... In all seriousness, I'd love to see employers offer more concierge services to reduce the mental load of all of the logistics and tasks at home that require time and phone calls to coordinate. With 10 hours of meetings a day, so much goes undone because I simply don't have time to stop and focus on it during business hours. Making doctor appointments, ordering birthday gifts, planning parties, buying school supplies and securing slots at summer camp, scheduling vacations...you name it! My 'mom brain' could focus so much more on work without all of those tasks floating around in my mind, taking up valuable space!"

Melanie Pickett, Executive Vice President at
large global bank and mom to 2

"I would change all systems that foster inequities for BIPOC (Black Indigenous and People of Color), women, LGBTQ+, and low-income families. Many policies, procedures, and benefits have been created with the intention to support but unintentionally have also created more harm. If I could wave a magic wand, I would move us from a capital-focused work system to a system that supports the health and well-being of all families. I would ensure that the focus is centered on those who have historically been marginalized for generations. Often during the development of systems, policies, and procedures a privileged decision-making lens is used versus the use of an equity lens. The use of an equity lens would allow for an intentionally and deliberately inclusive decision-making process which would help to ensure equity in process and outcomes."

Afra Smith, Founder & CEO of The Melanin Project

"Women carry 100% of the invisible expectation of managing children. Society needs to accept that everyone has a role handling those responsibilities."

Scott, COO of HardinDD

"If I could change one thing for working parents, it would be to break down the barriers of social media perfection and be real about raising kids. Raising kids is hard. It's expensive. It's exhausting. Sometimes I want to squeeze my five-year-old and tell her I love her so much it's painful. Sometimes I want to hide from my teenage foster child and pretend I'm still 25 and single. Sometimes my kids make me cry because they hurt my feelings or scream at me or tell me I'm a bad parent. Sometimes I would rather go to work than spend time with them. Sometimes I would rather clean the bathroom than play in the kitchen one more time. Admitting that they aren't my entire world and attributing my name to that admission is terrifying. What if someone finds out? What if someone judges me for my honesty?"

Allison Martinson, Training & Development
Manager, Mother & Foster Parent

"Make nearly all childcare costs tax deductible AND provide a tax credit for childcare for households with income under some threshold ($75,000?)."

Amy Rosenow, CEO of Fearless Financial and
mom of 2

"The world was set up to accept that moms work and want to be able to be a part of their kids' school and activities. It is very hard to do all of this really well."

Jessie S, Founder of The Improv Effect

"I think I'd want to change the societal perception that caring for kids is a mom's job. I don't need to tell you that dads get extra credit for parenting at all whereas moms are often made to feel inadequate for NOT parenting full time (while stay-at-home moms are made to feel inadequate for not working outside the home)."

Kieth Alperin, Tech Founder, Father of Two

"I would say the one thing I would change would be the emotional rollercoaster we go through as working moms. Feeling like we are constantly failing at work if we are with our kids or failing with our kids if we are at work is exhausting. I genuinely feel this comes from a social stigma that has hovered over us for many years."

Ashley Murphy, Co-Founder and CEO of Neat Method (and her family)

"Oftentimes our lives are full of little tasks that eat away at our day, week, and month. I would like to incorporate a separate employer budget and/or tax credit to be used for household services in order to give working parents more quality time for themselves and their families. These services could include things like cleaning, grocery shopping, a morning one-hour housekeeping service to unload the dishwasher, make the beds, do a load of laundry, walk the dog, etc. These are all things that have to be done, but I would rather take a walk in the park with my daughters, play a family board game, have a meaningful conversation or simply take a few minutes to meditate or work out."

Joanna Mirov, CEO of MXOtech

"I went through a slew of potential federal, state, and company policy changes in my mind, before I realized all were practical, not magical (at least if you look globally). So if I could use magic, I would do simply this: abolish the feeling of guilt in working parents. No guilt about parenting. No guilt about working. No guilt about wearing dirty sweatpants and just trying to make it through another day. If we could all collectively believe in ourselves, value parenting, and appreciate how hard it can be, we could cut ourselves some much needed slack, I think."

Amanda Lannert, CEO of Jellyvision, Mother of Many and Only Daughters

"Family first flex time—do what you need to do as the governing rule on PTO. Get your work done and if family demands shift your ability to deliver ontime, negotiate and collaborate."

Len, President, Husband, Dad of 2

"Stop the shaming and guilt for being a parent while working and building your career. Home life used to be at home, work at work, but with more women in the workforce and more men helping at home, the lines have blurred between home and work life, and I'd love it to be embraced. There's no such thing as work/life balance... It is one life, and we need to manage our priorities as they change through different phases of parenthood and building our careers. I'm building an "and" life... I'm an awesome and dedicated mama AND a diligent and energetic leader in my career... Let's encourage working parents to be both and not shame them for whatever phase they're in."

Laura, Leader, Engineer, and Mom of 2

"True understanding from leaders and team members without kids! Even the most supportive of teammates and managers cannot TRULY understand all the things we are juggling without having the actual experience of working parenthood."

Louisa, Mom of 2, Tax Practice Leader at Fine Point Consulting

Acknowledgments

I would like to thank all the people who contributed to this book, especially my publisher, Networlding, and the phenomenal coach, Melissa G Wilson: Your enthusiasm and encouragement were rocket fuel in the early days and in the last mile. My editor, Madelyn Sutton: Your insight is brilliant and I'm so fortunate to have worked with you!

My special thanks to Lorelei and Jennifer, who have been a wonderful sounding-board for years. I treasure your guidance, mentorship, and support.

To incredible friends, Sam Lee, Joanna and the Brauds, Meghann and the Dames, Audrey, Amanda, Sarah, Lisa, Megan, Tracey, Leah Roe, Sarah, Colleen, Brandies, Stefanie, and every powerhouse woman I know: thank you for always lifting as you rise!

To my mother, Toni, the OG Executive Mother and ultimate mentor. I'm so lucky to have your guidance and love. Thank you for blazing the trail. To my father, Jeff, thank you for sharing your stories and the secrets to success. I enjoy listening even though I've heard them once or twice before. I hope you are both well-pleased. To Creighton, thank you for being the best little bother a sister could ask for.

Thank you, Sean, for everything, but especially for making a life with me. It's better than I ever thought it could be.

To my children, Jeffrey and Annabelle. It's all for you.

Before You Go

It has been an honor and a pleasure sharing my experiences as a working mother. My goal was to help you and others find joy in your personal life and success in your professional life, without sacrificing one for the other. I hope the time you spent reading this book energizes you and propels you forward. The world needs you and the big impact you have to make.

Before you go, I have a request for a little more of your time, to help others who are trying to navigate the knowledge economy find this book. If what you read was helpful, in any way, would you be so kind as to leave a review on Amazon?

Please look up this title, *Executive Motherhood*, at www.Amazon.com, and write a brief review of how this book helped you. Even if you read only one or two chapters, you could mention why those insights helped you on your parenting journey, or something you might avoid doing in the future. Books like this are buried unless kind, generous readers, like you, take the time to post honest reviews. When reviews are posted, the algorithms take note and promote the book to other potential readers.

Thank you in advance for this generous expression of your appreciation. Your review will encourage me to spend more time sharing my advice with the public in this way. Being able to help others through writing means everything to me.

Also, please reach out to get in contact with me with any questions you might have through my email at ashley@ashleyquintopowell.com or through my website at www.ashleyquintopowell.com. To learn more about hiring a virtual assistant, visit us at www.myva.rocks. And to engage with the larger community of executive mothers, visit us at www.executivemotherhood.com.

I'm also available for speaking engagements and coaching. I look forward to hearing from you.

Printed in Great Britain
by Amazon